RUDOLF STEINER (1861–1925) called his spiritual philosophy 'anthroposophy', meaning 'wisdom of the human being'. As a highly developed seer, he based his work on direct knowledge and perception of spiritual dimensions. He initiated a modern and universal 'science of spirit', accessible to anyone willing to exercise clear and unprejudiced thinking.

From his spiritual investigations Steiner provided suggestions for the renewal of many activities, including education (both general and special), agriculture, medicine, economics, architecture, science, philosophy, religion and the arts. Today there are thousands of schools, clinics, farms and other organizations involved in practical work based on his principles. His many published works feature his research into the spiritual nature of the human being, the evolution of the world and humanity, and methods of personal development. Steiner wrote some 30 books and delivered over 6,000 lectures across Europe. In 1924 he founded the General Anthroposophical Society, which today has branches throughout the world.

SECRET BROTHERHOODS

SECRET BROTHERHOODS
and the Mystery of the
Human Double

Seven lectures given in St Gallen, Zurich and
Dornach between 6 and 25 November 1917

RUDOLF STEINER

RUDOLF STEINER PRESS

Translated by Johanna Collis

Rudolf Steiner Press
Hillside House, The Square
Forest Row, RH18 5ES

www.rudolfsteinerpress.com

First English edition 2004
Reprinted 2006, 2011

Originally published in German, with two additional lectures, under the
title *Individuelle Geistwesen und ihr Wirken in der Seele des Menschen*
(volume 178 in the *Rudolf Steiner Gesamtausgabe* or Collected Works) by
Rudolf Steiner Verlag, Dornach. (The lectures of 10 and 11 November
1917 are available in English in *Freud, Jung and Spiritual Psychology*,
Anthroposophic Press.) This authorized translation, based on the 4th
edition, is published by permission of the Rudolf Steiner
Nachlassverwaltung, Dornach

Translation © Rudolf Steiner Press 2004

A catalogue record for this book is available from the British Library

ISBN 978 1 85584 162 8

Cover by Andrew Morgan
Typeset by DP Photosetting, Aylesbury, Bucks.
Printed and bound by Gutenberg Press, Malta

MIX
Paper from
responsible sources
FSC
www.fsc.org   FSC® C022612

The paper used for this book is FSC-certified and
totally chlorine-free. FSC (the Forest Stewardship
Council) is an international network to promote
responsible management of the world's forests.

Contents

Lecture Summaries   ix

Introduction *by Terry Boardman*   xiii

1. Knowledge of the Supersensible and Riddles of
   the Human Soul
   Public Lecture, St Gallen, 15 November 1917   1

2. The Mystery of the Double. Geographic Medicine
   St Gallen, 16 November 1917   44

3. Behind the Scenes of External Events, I
   Zurich, 6 November 1917   77

4. Behind the Scenes of External Events, II
   Zurich 13 November 1917   100

5. Individual Spirit Beings and the Constant
   Foundation of the Universe, I
   Dornach, 18 November 1917   127

6. Individual Spirit Beings and the Constant
   Foundation of the Universe, II
   Dornach, 19 November 1917   153

7. Individual Spirit Beings and the Constant
   Foundation of the Universe, III
   Dornach, 25 November 1917   175

Notes   197

Index of Names   211

Note regarding Rudolf Steiner's Lectures   213

Lecture Summaries

Lecture 1
Characterization of science and spiritual science: scientific observation traces phenomena back to their origin (birth) and studies what is visible; the starting-point for spiritual science is death and what happens thereafter in the spiritual world. Resignation or the courage to seek more knowledge when the outer limits are reached. F. T. Vischer. Du Bois-Reymond. Inner and outer pictures. Calculations by James Dewar and those based on the Kant-Laplace theory. Forces of construction (life) and destruction (death). Imagination, Inspiration, Intuition. How the manner of death affects the next life. Understanding the soul and spirit elements in human being and universe. How spiritual knowledge illumines destiny. The effects on life and life after death of materialistic and spiritual world views. Darwin, Haeckel, Hartmann, Hertwig. Goetheanism.

Lecture 2
The time has come to reveal spiritual secrets. Increasing emphasis on materialism since the sixteenth century necessitates the search for spiritual knowledge today. The importance of a shared cultivation of spiritual science for the life of the soul after death. Spiritual concepts throw light on knowledge. How the spiritual world impinges on the physical. The faculty of love. The double entering before birth and wanting to remain after death. This has been prevented by the Mystery of Golgotha, as is known to secret brotherhoods and must now become known to all. Geographic medicine and how the double is affected by emanations from the

earth. European contacts with America before and after the age of the consciousness soul. Christianization by Irish and Scottish missionaries. The earth as a living organism. Nationalism and world culture. Russia and America. Europe's relationship with America; Emerson and Woodrow Wilson. Spiritual science as a force for life.

Lecture 3

Human souls now becoming conscious of much that formerly lay beyond consciousness. Some are concerned more with the spiritual world while others seek earthly power. The guidance of humanity in accordance with esoteric laws. Becoming conscious of the mysteries of sickness, procreation and death. Knowledge gained by souls who die by assassination. The power of secret brotherhoods. Efforts to paralyse spiritual development. The important year of 1841. The spirits of darkness at work in human souls since 1879. Seeing through them robs them of their power. Working for spiritual science.

Lecture 4

The transformation of soul life during the course of time. Monotheism leads human beings only to their own angel. Personal monotheism leads to national monotheism. Instead, one ought to enter into a concrete relationship with the spiritual world. Reality must prevail over abstraction. The battle in the spiritual world between 1841 and 1879. The spirits of darkness at work. Secret brotherhoods and their various goals. The task of spiritual science. How materialistic views work in the spiritual world. The nature of freedom. Relationship with the dead. Psychoanalysis. Disorders of the soul as a consequence of a wrong relationship with the dead. Spiritual knowledge as a remedy. Working out of spiritual impulses and the obstacles encountered.

Lecture 5

The spirit cannot be comprehended by means of the concept of the unconscious. Where there is spirit there is consciousness.

Secret brotherhoods seek to use occult knowledge for their own ends. The zenith of materialism and experiencing the appearance of Christ in the etheric. To tackle evil consciously is a contemporary task. How spiritual or materialistic concepts work in the life after death, and how secret brotherhoods use this knowledge. The illusion that spiritual forces are merely forces of nature. Spiritualism — a higher form of materialism. A protection against occult machinations is to recognize them. The Christ-impulse. The inclination of western and eastern secret brotherhoods to distract human souls from the appearance of Christ. The impulse of Ireland. Eliminating the 'American' impulse. The subconscious and the double. The latter's dependence on terrestrial conditions.

Lecture 6
The secret brotherhoods and spiritualism. Contradictions in life. A unifying universal principle and how certain spiritual individualities work. Living reality and abstract lack of contradiction. Outer nature suggests the existence of a unifying universal principle, but individual spirits contradict one another behind the tapestry of the senses. The elemental beings. Thinking, feeling and will and how differentiated beings work. Evil. Christ in the fifth post-Atlantean period. Freedom. The legend of Ireland. Ireland and the Christianization of Europe. The double and freedom. Taylor's division of labour as an example.

Lecture 7
The old culture is gone and spiritual science points to the future. Vital questions: Use of etheric forces in machines. Control of life, sickness and death. Control of procreation and birth. Forces coming in from points in the zodiac. To overlook spiritual impulses or take hold of them in freedom. The philosophers' stone. God, virtue, immortality. How the secret brotherhoods redefine them. Selfless consideration of spiritual matters is a contemporary necessity. How western and eastern brotherhoods

use spiritual knowledge. Depending on how human beings behave on earth, the dead can work out of the spiritual world in freedom or be coerced into human existence in an artificial way.

Introduction
by Terry Boardman

This is a stark and extremely challenging group of lectures, given at a decisive time of tremendous crisis for humanity and dealing with themes that stretch from 1917 back into the distant past as well as into the far future. Johanna Collis's new translation is eminently readable and lucid, making the reader's task of getting to grips with the challenging nature of the content that much easier.

This publication of these lectures, originally given by Rudolf Steiner in Dornach, Zurich, and St Gallen in November 1917, is timely indeed, for so many of the topics are of direct relevance to numerous difficult aspects of life in our own time. Steiner deals with: the drive towards a world government by elitist forces that seek to control the masses through the forces of economics, technology and political assassinations; the goals of secret brotherhoods in the West that work through these forces and other such brotherhoods in the East with their own aims and methods; the ways in which both these groups work against the Christ; the nature of the American continent and the forces that proceed from it; the relations between Russia, Europe and America; the meaning of Ireland for world development; the spiritual origin of electromagnetism; the relation between the life after death and life on the physical plane; the abuse of inoculations and vaccinations; the nature of the double, or doppelgänger, and the dangers of psychoanalysis; the confusion of angels with higher beings and the divinity; the difference between thinking and brain activity, and above all, the need for clear insight into world events that is based on spiritual knowledge. These are just some of the main themes in this remarkably illuminating collection of lectures, which, in a way, complement the lectures given in December 1916 and January 1917 (published in English as *The Karma of Untruthfulness*, Vols I and II). While in that earlier series of lectures at the beginning of the year 1917 Steiner went into very great detail about the specifics of world events related to the coming of the First World War (an effort to illuminate the past causes of the war), in these November lectures he paints on a much broader canvas and is looking more to the future in the light of what the war has revealed, especially in view of the dramatic events of the year 1917 itself. In these lectures he was giving his listeners important *strategic* keys with which the developments in the twentieth century and beyond could be illuminated.

Much has been said in recent years about the epoch-making significance of the events of 2001, notably that of 11 September, but historians in the future may well look back and judge that 1917 was a far more signficant year for humanity—the year in which, arguably, the twentieth century really began. The year 1917 was indeed a crucial one for the modern world and for Rudolf Steiner, as these lectures make clear.

He began the year by continuing the series of lectures he had commenced in Dornach in December 1916 on 'The Occult Background of the War', published in English under the title *The Karma of Untruthfulness*, Vols I and II. Given at a critical point in the war when at Christmas 1916 there was the best hope for peace negotiations following formal peace proposals put forward by the German and American governments, those remarkable lectures were akin to a crash course in applied media studies and world events for an anthroposophical membership who, he felt, had been too interested in hearing only about the spiritual world and not so much about the relations between the spiritual and material worlds that had resulted in the catastrophe of the war. The peace moves of December 1916 offered perhaps the last real hope for sanity and peace. The month proved to be the hinge on which the war turned. The Western Allies rejected the vague German peace offers of Christmas 1916 out of hand, and on 6 April President Woodrow Wilson took the United States into the First World War. On 11 March the British captured Baghdad from the Turks and on the following day, the Russian Revolution ended the 300-year-old rule of the Romanovs. The first American troops arrived in Europe in June. From May to October 'visions' of the Virgin Mary were seen at Fatima, one of which on 13 July spoke about the need for the conversion of Russia. On 1 August at the same time as a lecture course Rudolf Steiner gave in Berlin on the Karma of Materialism, Pope Benedict XV, in a vain attempt to wield the influence of the Roman Catholic Church, issued his seven-point peace plan to the belligerents, which was ignored by all except Austria-Hungary. During the summer the revolutionary republican government led by Alexander Kerensky in Russia crumbled, and at the very time Rudolf Steiner was giving the lectures in the present collection, the Bolsheviks seized power on 7 November. Two days later the British Government's Balfour Declaration to Lord Rothschild was published, which promised a national home in Palestine for the Jewish people. On the Western Front, the appalling slaughter and macabre horrors of the Third Battle of Ypres (Passchendaele) had just dragged to its end on the day

Steiner gave the first of these lectures. It had begun, back on 18 July, with a British artillery bombardment from 3000 guns firing four and a quarter million shells that lasted for ten days. British and German casualties numbered some 600,000 after the three months of the 'battle' — such was the karma of European materialism, the direct result, as Rudolf Steiner puts it, of too many people having been asleep both to world events prior to 1914 and to the ways in which spiritual realities play into those events.

After the lectures in the present collection, Rudolf Steiner gave in Dornach a course of seven lectures in December of this fateful year 1917 that concerned themselves with historical necessity and free will. During that course, on 11 December, the first 'Christian' army for 673 years entered Jerusalem under the British General Allenby, a direct descendant of Oliver Cromwell. On 23 December in Basel, Rudolf Steiner gave a lecture, later published under the title *Et Incarnatus Est, The Time-Cycle in Historical Events*, in which he presented the vital key for historical understanding of the 33-year periodicity in historical events that is based on the life of Jesus Christ.

Britain, France, Germany, Austria-Hungary, the Vatican — all the old European powers proved themselves in 1917 to be utterly bankrupt of new and fruitful ideas that could lead the Continent out of the morass of the war and into some kind of healing process. The karma of European materialism, especially since 1841–79, had led to the result that Europe's 300-year period of global domination was about to be overwhelmed by the massive forces of the peripheral superpowers of America and Russia, whose mutual enmity would overshadow the rest of the twentieth century and threaten to extinguish European culture altogether.

Any good public speaker is always very aware of the time and space in which a lecture is being given. A good public speaker who also happens to be clairvoyant can go further and be aware of the individuals in the audience who will—as a result of their special interests and destiny—be especially receptive to the content of the lecture. It is never an easy matter to determine why Rudolf Steiner gave a particular lecture on a particular date at a particular place or why he chose to insert a particular section or even a particular sentence in a lecture that might, on a superficial reading of it, seem odd or out of place. One of the points he makes in this collection of lectures is that those who communicate spiritual ideas to the wider public must be prepared for many disappointments. They must realize that out of an audience of scores or hundreds, only one or two may be really open for what is being given. Only one or two lives may be changed by it, if any. Nevertheless one must press on with the work regardless, with iron determination, understanding that spiritual reality is mirrored in natural reality; just as nature is amazingly fecund and only a few seeds in a season may actually survive to become fully grown plants, so the speaker on spiritual realities must be aware that in the audience in the specific location where the lecture is being given there may be just the right individual(s) who will really be able to make something of what is being said.

As a clairvoyant researcher, Rudolf Steiner was in a position to know these things, so that when he gave some of the lectures in this collection, those in St Gallen and Zurich, for example, he was aware that in St Gallen he was speaking in a location where the early Celtic Christian monks of Ireland with their strong impulse for healing had been active during the Dark Ages. He was aware that some of those Celtic Christian missionaries to the Continent knew of the existence of America and of the need to keep Europe 'walled off' spiritually from America until Europe was ready to deal with the powerful spiritual forces related to the American continent. These forces had a purely geographic nature connected to subterranean magnetism and the north-south axis of mountain ranges such as the Rockies and the Andes. Spiritual knowledge of this fact by Europeans with insight led to visits to the American continent to do special research into medicines that could only be done on the American continent. Was it merely coincidence that one who carried the same name as the Irish Celtic missionary Columbanus and who hailed from Italy, the land where Columbanus died, found the way to America 1100 years after Columbanus and the Celtic Christians had, according to Rudolf Steiner in these lectures, been responsible for assisting Rome in cutting Europe off from America?

Steiner was also aware, as he says in lecture 4 of this collection, that in his own day Zurich was a strong centre for the modern practice of psychoanalysis, a practice he describes as extremely 'dangerous' because it was attempting to deal with powerful spiritual forces operative in the subconscious without understanding the very real nature of those forces. Later in the twentieth century, Zurich, with its infamous 'gnomes', and Basel, home of the central bankers' bank (the Bank of International Settlements), would become centres of global financial control closely linked to London and New York.

This relates to another in the trio of main themes in these lectures: the clandestine efforts of secretive oligarchical brotherhoods to exercise a control over the masses of humanity that is historically illegitimate in the post-

Renaissance, post-Reformation modern epoch—a control that is based on influencing the subconscious by means of instilling fear, for example, the kind of economic fear that proceeds today mainly from the Western world. The activities of these secretive elitist groups that work through modern capitalism and technology create juggernaut-like forces that produce a counteraction of fear in others, who may be members of traditional non-Western societies that feel their cultures threatened. They may be idealistic people in Western societies whose feelings and instincts are in the right direction for the modern age but whose thinking and insight are unable to cope with events. Both of these two different types of groups can then lash out in forms of terrorism at what they feel to be oppression.

Whereas normal development in the modern age ought to take place in accordance with the conscious under-standing of the autonomous individual, Steiner shows in these lectures how esoteric groups seek to perpetuate the methods of past epochs when societies were led, flocklike, by the initiates of the mystery centres. Furthermore, actions that were once justified in the right historical context have become evil, he says, in that these power-hungry elite groups are now serving spiritual beings who have been particularly active within human thinking (in what can well up from the subconscious) since the last third of the nine-teenth century and which seek to extinguish all spiritual life and replace it with a thoroughgoing materialism, aiming to cut off the possibility of human contact with the Christ. One of the ways in which they do this, Rudolf Steiner reveals, is by making use of the dead in ritualistic fashion; those who cross the threshold of death through murder or assassina-tion can thereby learn things which those who cross over in normal ways do not, and the secret brotherhoods can acquire this knowledge from the dead by means of mediums and rituals. Steiner's research here opens up an avenue for how to reconsider events of mass killing such as the Tokyo underground gas attacks or the deaths of nearly 3000 people in the attacks on the Twin Towers. What happens to the dead when they go over the threshold in such a way as the result of willed murderous action that emanates from groups with specific political or cultural aims? Indeed, the topic of relations between the living and the dead, especially in terms of manipulation of the dead and of the thoughts of the dead, is a main theme of these lectures, which were given between 6 and 25 November, traditionally the season for remembrance of the dead. It is noteworthy that in the first lecture in the collection Steiner starkly points out that spiritual science must take its starting-point from the fact of death and the limits it appears to impose. Death and its role in the scheme of things must be understood. Without understanding of the relation between death and life, without going beyond the limits that death appears to present, says Rudolf Steiner, we will be at a loss to comprehend the real nature of many events in the modern world.

In these lectures Rudolf Steiner shows the relation of 1917 to the Fall of the Spirits of Darkness, the dark angels who were cast out of the spiritual world in 1879 following the long 'War in Heaven' that began in 1841. He draws attention to the actions of power groups serving these beings in east and west in 1917. 'Awareness alone ... clear recognition and understanding' of spiritual realities together with willingness to recognize the objective evil forces at work in the world *and their purpose in the scheme of things* — these are the only means that can be of real help in modern humanity's predicament, says Steiner. These capacities of

awareness, recognition and understanding of spritual realities lead to what in modern parlance has come to be called
'consciousness raising', and that is a real power, because, as
Rudolf Steiner points out in these lectures of nearly 90 years
ago, the idea that 'you are what you eat' is a lie. *The fact is
that both in life and after death we actually become what we think:*
if we choose to think that we are animals, entirely materialistic beings concerned essentially with survival, as many
of today's neo-Darwinist evolutionary biologists and
sociobiologists would have us believe, then that is what we
will become. It should be obvious to anyone that this is
actually taking place before our eyes today, as some people
actually attempt to turn themselves into lizards or cyborgs,
seeking to turn parts of their bodies into animal forms or to
incorporate various technological devices into them, from
robot limbs to brain implants and infra-red vision.

Again and again, when confronted by the many serious
problems with which humanity has been struggling since
the First World War and is still facing, the almost despairing
question is often asked, even in anthroposophical circles:
'What can I do? What can the individual do about the
machinations of these secret groups, if indeed they exist?
It's all too much for individuals.' Rudolf Steiner's answer in
these lectures is bold and clear:

> The only defence against these things is knowing about
> them. If you know about them, you are protected ... But
> you must not be idle about acquiring real knowledge of
> these things.

The old word of the New Testament, 'Repent!' — *metanoia* —
change your thinking and raise your consciousness and that
of your fellows—such is the challenging call of these lectures given at the birth crisis of the twentieth century.

1. Knowledge of the Supersensible and Riddles of the Human Soul

Tracing how the human spirit evolves across the centuries and millennia leads to a sense of how it progresses step by step ever and again to new and yet more new achievements in the field of knowledge as well as in the field of action. Perhaps one should not place too much emphasis on the word 'progress' as such, since this might raise serious doubts in certain connections in view of the tragic times that have befallen humanity just now. But apart from this it must surely be obvious to all those who are interested in the evolution of the human spirit that the forms in which this spirit casts its efforts undergo radical changes over the course of centuries. In what I want to put before you today we shall strive to understand something new that wants to enter into human evolution, so we shall be helped by comparing this with other situations in which similarly new elements came into conflict with older views and had difficulty in taking hold as humanity evolved.

How difficult it was, for example, to establish the validity of the Copernican view of the world in the face of people's habits of thought and feeling;[1] in the case of certain aspects it took centuries to establish this view, which broke with what people had for ages considered to be the truth about the structure of their universe based on what they could see with their own eyes. A time had come when they could no longer rely on what their eyes told them about how the sun moved, rising and then setting again. In opposition to what they saw they had to concede that the sun stood still, at least in its relation to the earth. People's established habits of thinking and feeling do not fit in easily with such revolutions in knowledge.

In the case of the spiritual science of anthroposophy, which is to be the subject of this evening's talk, we are dealing with an even greater turnaround. There are good and firm scientific grounds for being convinced that the content of this spiritual science, too, must now take its place in the further evolution of human thinking and feeling. In the hope that you will not be offended I would like to begin by introducing this subject as follows.

The Copernican world view, like many other things, was opposed by countless prejudices and traditional opinions because people believed that if they were to replace them by something else this would spell the end of all kinds of religious ideas and so on. But in the case of what I shall be speaking about this evening a great deal more is rising up as well. It is here not only a matter of the kind of prejudices that stood against the Copernican world view. The problem here is that very many people in our time, the majority in fact, people who consider themselves to be enlightened and well educated, are raising up more than their prejudices and assumptions in opposition, for these enlightened and well educated individuals quite simply feel embarrassed to enter in all seriousness into the realms of which anthroposophy has to speak. They feel they are letting themselves down not only in front of those around them but in front of themselves if they admit that it is possible to gain knowledge regarding the subject we shall be discussing today that is just as scientific as knowledge regarding external nature and its structures; they feel they are making fools of themselves or behaving childishly in their own eyes.

These are the factors that have to be taken into account when speaking today about the spiritual science of anthroposophy. Someone speaking about this science on the basis of real knowledge about it is only too familiar with the hundredfold, even thousandfold, objections that are raised. Such a person is familiar with the objections simply because it is not only the separate truths and results of this spiritual science which are doubted but the very fact that there can be any true knowledge about the realm with which the spiritual science of anthroposophy is concerned. Very many people still regard it as entirely justifiable to develop beliefs, general beliefs about the realm of the eternal in the human soul. But when it comes to facts not understood in the world of the senses, facts pertaining to what is immortal and eternal in human nature, then those who form their judgements on the basis of our perfectly valid present-day scientific thinking regard as mainly fantasy and visionary nonsense the statement that actual factual knowledge can be gained about such things.

Well, this evening we shall not be dealing with any fantasy or visionary nonsense but with a realm that may well put off many, especially those who consider themselves to be scientific in their thinking. But first let me also briefly mention that the spiritual science of anthroposophy has no intention of being in any way sectarian. Anyone assuming that it is intended to be the foundation of some sort of new religious denomination is entirely mistaken as to its nature. As it is today, anthroposophy is a necessary consequence of what scientific progress has produced by way of a world view, a general, even popular world view held by the widest circles of humanity. This scientific progress that has yielded so many concepts on which the world view of the widest circles is based, concepts which are in turn the source of feelings and sentiments, this scientific way of looking at the world has assumed the task of exploring and explaining whatever can be detected by our external senses, whatever natural laws about facts observable by the outer senses can be comprehended by the human mind.

Even if we pay attention only to the realm of life — things are more obscure in other realms, but the realm of life shows up the matter very clearly — then we can see how in every case science must endeavour to work its way back to the origins, to whatever is the original seed for what grows and comes into being, for whatever flourishes. When scientists want to give their own explanation of animal or human life they look back to birth; they study embryology, they study whatever it is out of which something that is growing emerges. Science goes right back to the beginning of what can be perceived by the senses, namely, birth. Or, if it wants to explain the world as a whole, then it goes back, via various hypotheses based on geology, palaeontology or whatever the various branches of science have to offer, to what can be imagined as regards the birth of the world's whole structure. Although one individual or another may have expressed doubts as to the justification for such a way of thinking, nevertheless it is this thinking that has always been applied. We know what ideas have been put forward in the attempt to penetrate if not to the very beginning of earth's existence then at least to far distant periods of evolution, for example those when man did not yet exist on the earth; we know what has been put forward to explain in some measure how what came afterwards as the perceptible world human beings have around them emerged from what was there before in seed form. Darwin's theory[2] or, if you want to leave that out of account, the theory of evolution as such, all such theories stand on discovering how something that comes into being arises out of something that was there before. Wherever you look the effort is made to go back to younger times and birth.

The spiritual science of anthroposophy occupies a different position. Its point of departure is the very thing that initially engenders objections without people realizing this fully. The objections are unclear, they could be termed subconscious or instinctive. And such objections are often far more effective than those which are clearly recognized and thought through. In order to reach clear ideas, not vague generalities about spiritual concepts but actual spiritual facts, the spiritual science of anthroposophy has to make death its point of departure. From the start it thus finds itself in fundamental opposition to the favoured manner of proceeding today when birth and youth, growth and forward steps in development are the point of departure. Death intervenes in life. Wherever you look in scientific literature today you will find that conscientious researchers consider it impossible to see death as such as a scientific concept.

Yet the scientist of the spirit has to regard death, that which comes to an end and is the opposite of birth, as his starting-point. For him the fundamental question to be asked is: how does death and whatever is connected with it intervene in life in the wider sense? Death brings to an end whatever the senses can perceive; death dissolves what comes into being and what evolves in full view of the senses. Death intervenes like something we imagine to be unconcerned with what is at work here in the sense-perceptible world where everything flourishes, springs up and lives. So the view arises, wrongly but to some extent quite understandably, that we can know nothing about what death covers up and hides.

This is the facet of human feeling which leads to all the counter-arguments that can of course be raised against the results of what is, after all, still a young science. It is indeed still a young science, and for the reasons just mentioned the spiritual scientist, even when speaking about the discoveries of his science, finds himself in a situation quite different from that of the natural scientist. The spiritual scientist cannot proceed in the same way as the natural scientist who states a fact and then proves it on the basis of the conviction that people can see it with their own eyes. The spiritual scientist speaks about things that cannot be perceived with the senses. Therefore when speaking about the results of his research he is always obliged to indicate how these results are achieved.

There is now a rich vein of literature on the realm about which I shall be speaking to you this evening. Even though they thereby merely prove how inaccurately and superficially they read, critics who feel called upon to complain, for example about what I have written, keep on maintaining that this scientist of the spirit makes statements which he does not prove. Well, dear members of the audience, he does bring proof, but he does so in a different way. He begins by describing how he has reached his conclusions, for he first has to show the path by which he has entered into the realm of these facts. This path in itself is often off-putting because it is unfamiliar to present-day habits of thinking and feeling. Although the spiritual scientist does not reject the methods by which natural science reaches its brilliant results but rather admires them greatly, the very nature of his research leads him to the inescapable conclusion that those methods cannot serve as a means by which to enter the supersensible realm.

Indeed, the spiritual scientist finds his point of departure in the very experience of how limited the procedures of that scientific thinking are. When natural science reaches the final boundary of knowledge in a certain area, what so often happens nowadays is that people simply say: 'Here we have reached the limit of what human beings can know.' Spiritual science, however, endeavours to use this very limit to come to certain experiences which can only be attained at such boundaries. I have specifically discussed these boundaries of human knowing in my book *Von Seelenrätseln* (Riddles of the soul) which is being published just now.[3]

Those who have not taken knowledge to be something that just happens to land on them from outside but who have wrestled with knowledge and with truth, such people have always had certain experiences when coming up against their outer limits. But times are changing and human evolution is going through transformations. Even quite recently the most outstanding thinkers and wrestlers with knowledge fetched up at these outer limits with the attitude that they could go no further, that this was where they would have to come to a halt. Those of you who have heard me speak a few times will know that it is rarely my habit to touch on personal matters. But since personal experience is here bound up with what I am trying to put forward I hope you will allow me to do so on this occasion. I have to say that what I want to explain about these experiences at the outer limits of knowledge is founded on more than 30 years of continuous spiritual research. It was over 30 years ago that these problems and tasks, these riddles that arise at the outer limits of knowledge, first made a strong impression on me.

There are many examples I could quote regarding these boundaries, but let me mention one which was pointed out by a genuine wrestler with knowledge: Friedrich Theodor Vischer, the well-known aesthete who was also a most important philosopher although during his lifetime he was too little recognized and soon forgotten.[4] Several decades ago Vischer wrote a very interesting discourse on a very interesting book on imagination in dreams by Volkelt.[5] He mentioned a number of things which need not concern us here, but there is one sentence one might easily fail to notice but which, on the other hand, could strike the soul like a bolt of lightning if that soul were filled with the desire for knowledge and were truly struggling inwardly for real knowledge. It is a sentence that occurred to Vischer as he pondered and wondered about the nature of the human soul. Thinking about what science had had to say about the human being in recent times he deduced: It is quite clear that this human soul cannot be solely within the body; but it is equally clear that it cannot be outside the body either.[6]

We are here confronted with a complete contradiction, one that cannot easily be solved. It is a contradiction that must of necessity present itself to someone who is seriously concerned with the struggle for knowledge. The time had not yet arrived when it would have been possible for Vischer to push on from that limit of ordinary knowledge to an inner experience of such a contradiction. Even today, from most of those seeking knowledge, we still hear what occurs to them when they come up against such a contradiction—and there are hundreds and hundreds of such contradictions, like the seven riddles of the universe mentioned by Du Bois-Reymond, that witty physiologist.[7] What those seeking knowledge today continue to say is: This is as far as human knowledge can go; it cannot get beyond this point. This is said by these individuals because when they reach a limit of human knowledge they cannot bring themselves to make the step from mere thinking, mere inner pictures, to actual experience.

The place to begin is where such a contradiction brings us up short, not one that we have cleverly thought out ourselves but one that is revealed to us by the universal riddles. We must try to live continuously with that contradiction, wrestling with it time and again as we do with ordinary problems in life; indeed we must immerse ourselves in it with our whole soul. We have to muster the courage of thinking and with this immerse ourselves in the contradiction without fearing that it might shatter the picture formations in our soul or that our soul might not be capable of taking the next step. In my book *Von Seelenrätseln* I have quite recently described in detail this wrestling that must take place at those outer limits of knowledge.

We can make progress when we arrive at one of these boundaries with all the fullness of our soul rather than merely with the ideas we manufacture or cleverly work out and fix for ourselves. Our progress is not merely a matter of logic, for it is on the path of living knowledge that we then proceed. I shall have to use a comparison to describe what we experience there, for the path of spiritual research is a genuine experience of knowledge, a fact of knowledge, and language does not yet have many expressions for such things since our words only serve for external perceptions brought to us by our senses. So what we see quite clearly before our spiritual eyes can only be expressed by means of a comparison.

When we enter in a living way into a contradiction of the kind we are speaking about we feel as though we have reached a barrier, a barrier at which the spiritual world not found in the sense-perceptible world is knocking as though from the outside. It does not matter if the picture I want to use is not entirely accurate scientifically, for it is sufficient for use as a means of comparison. It is as though a living creature of a primitive order which has not yet evolved a sense of touch were to experience inwardly through constant inward movements the barriers of the physical world and the surfaces of separate objects. A creature that has not yet evolved a sense of touch but which experiences the surfaces of things in this way is as yet still entirely enclosed within itself; it cannot as yet feel by means of touch what is outside it in the way of sense-perceptible impressions.

This is how someone who wrestles with knowledge feels — entirely in the sphere of spirit and soul, and certainly not in any material way — when he arrives at a borderline place such as I have just described. When the organism of a primitive creature breaks through like this it becomes differentiated out into an organ for the sense of touch as the result of colliding with the sense-perceptible world outside it; it can then feel the surfaces and know whether they are rough or smooth, hot or cold; it opens up what is inside it to what is outside it. In a similar way one who wrestles with knowledge can break through a boundary and acquire a spiritual organ of touch. Having wrestled perhaps for many years to break through into the spiritual world at a boundary of knowledge we come to a point where we gain real spiritual organs. This is only a very elementary description of how such a sense of touch can develop. If I may use certain expressions by giving them a fuller meaning: out of our state of being enclosed within ourselves we can develop spiritual eyes and spiritual ears if we work and work at this ever and ever again.

Many today still find it absurd to speak of the soul being

initially as undifferentiated as the organism of a primitive creature and of it being able to form its senses out of its own substance, so that out of that substance soul instruments, differentiated soul organs can be formed for perceiving the spirit, organs which then confront the soul with the spiritual world.

But the time has now come when it can be said that spiritual science, presented scientifically with full justification, is entering in a new way into the progress of knowledge which human evolution is undergoing. This is not entirely new in all respects, for we can see how especially the most outstanding searchers for knowledge sought and strove to attain spiritual knowledge in past times. Just now I mentioned Friedrich Theodor Vischer. Let us hear him describe in his own words how he came to stand before one of those outer limits of knowledge, how he stopped there without crossing it; how he did not make the transition from that inner stirring to the breakthrough which would have given him a spiritual sense of touch. I shall read you the passage where he describes how in wrestling with the riddles of science he reached one of those places where the spiritual world hammers at the door of the human soul. This happened at a time when materialistic science was presenting serious seekers for knowledge with numerous riddles which led many to say that the only way to view the soul was to see it as nothing but a product of physical effects.

Here are his words:[8] 'No spirit where there is no nerve centre, where there is no brain, say the opponents. No nerve centre, no brain, say we, if countless stages have not prepared it from below. It is easy to jest about a rumbling of spirit in granite or limestone; no harder than it would be for us to ask mockingly how it is possible for the protein in the brain to rise up and produce ideas. Yet how those stages might be measured escapes human understanding. We cannot fathom how spirit can produce nature as a counterstroke so perfect that to knock against it gives us bruises.'

Note, please, how this man who is wrestling for knowledge describes us as being bruised in the process; here you have the inner experience of one who, in wrestling for knowledge, is having to hammer away at it.

Vischer continues: 'And here we come to a fundamental parting of the ways from any such apparent metaphysical Absolute, since the Hegelian formulations—"being other than itself" and "being outside itself", witty, perhaps, but with little meaning—merely disguise the radical nature of the dividing wall which we seem to have come up against. In Fichte due recognition is given to the cut and thrust implicit in this "counterstroke" that stands over against the spirit, but it is not really explained.'

Here we have a description by someone who is wrestling for knowledge at a time when it was not yet possible for the decision, the decision of spiritual science, to be taken to go beyond the stroke and counterstroke and break right through the dividing wall that separates us from the spiritual world. I can only speak about these things in general here, but you can find detailed descriptions in my books. Specifically in *How to Know Higher Worlds*[9] and the second part of *An Outline of Esoteric Science*[10] you will find detailed descriptions of the inner agility and exercises the soul will have to practise—if I may be allowed this expression—in order to transform its undifferentiated state into spiritual organs which can then perceive the spiritual world.

Much has to be done if one wants to follow this path of

genuine research. Much has to be done because in our time habits of thought have evolved in the field of scientific study which, while being fully appropriate for this field, amount to a specific way of thinking that is the opposite of the ways of thinking that lead into the spiritual world. It is therefore perfectly understandable that the pronouncements which come from the scientific angle show no wish to understand the spiritual world as it really is with all its facts.

The one thing I want to say here — for as I have said, you will find detailed descriptions in the books just mentioned — is that people will have to strive for quite a different way of forming inner concepts. In ordinary life we are satisfied with concepts and inner pictures so long as they provide an image of some external fact or thing. But for spiritual research this is unsatisfactory. For the soul of the spiritual researcher inner pictures and concepts become something quite unlike those of today's ordinary habits of thought. Let me once again use a comparison to show how a spiritual researcher confronts the world today. Materialists, spiritualists, pantheists, monadists, all such people believe they can penetrate the riddles of the universe; by applying certain inner pictures or concepts they attempt to gain an idea of universal processes.[11]

This is not at all the way in which spiritual researchers regard concepts. For them, these have to be approached in the clear knowledge that in the external, sense-perceptible world concepts or inner pictures are no different from, say, a photograph taken of a tree or other object from one specific angle. A photograph taken from one angle gives you a picture from that angle while another taken from a different angle results in a different picture. From a third and fourth angle you get two further pictures. The pictures are all different, but together, when you combine them in your mind's eye, they give you an inner image of the complete tree. Yet it is easy to say that one picture contradicts the other, for things look very different depending on the angle from which the photographs are taken.

So for a spiritual researcher, all those ideas put forward by pantheists, monadists and so on are nothing more than different photographs of reality. Spiritual reality does not open itself to our life of ideas and concepts if we maintain that a concept is a true image, for we must go all round something and form many, many concepts about it from all angles. This enables us to develop a much more extensive and agile inner life of soul than we are used to having in the external world of the senses; it also means that we have to make concepts much more alive. They are then no longer mere copies, for by experiencing them we make them into something much more alive than ordinary life and the things in it.

Let me put this in another way. Think of a rose that has been cut from a rose-bush. Imagine it to yourself. When you make an inner picture of it you may often feel it to be something real, as if the rose were something real. A spiritual researcher, on the other hand, will never make progress by being satisfied that the rose is something real. A rose imagined all by itself with a short stalk is nothing real, for it can only exist if it is part of the rose-bush. It is the rose-bush that is real. So for all the separate items of which people make inner pictures for themselves, believing these to be something real, the spiritual researcher must be constantly aware of the limited degree to which such a thing is actually a reality. When imagining a rose with a stalk he must feel that it is not something real; he must sense and feel and experience the degree of unreality that is contained in this rose that is merely a single bloom.

By extending this to cover our whole way of viewing the world we cause our world of inner pictures to come alive. Instead of the paralysed, dead inner pictures with which science is satisfied today we gain inner pictures that are as alive as the things imagined. However, if we take today's habits of thought as our point of departure we shall at first be disappointed; there will be disappointments for us because what we experience will be so very different from the thought habits of today. It is unavoidable that what one says on the basis of knowledge of the spiritual world must sometimes sound rather paradoxical with regard to what is generally said and believed nowadays.

It is possible to be tremendously scholarly, let's say in physics. One can be immensely scholarly and much admired on account of one's scholarship while working with all kinds of concepts that have not been reached or worked on in the manner I have described which brings one's world of inner pictures to life. What I said was very elementary, but in a spiritual researcher this elementary work must encompass one's whole way of viewing the world. Let me give an example.

Earlier in this century Professor Dewar gave a very important lecture in London.[12] Every sentence of that lecture revealed a great scholar of the present time, one who is as thoroughly versed in the ideas of physics as anyone can possibly be. Based on the ideas of physics as they are at present, this professor endeavours to speak about the final condition of the earth, or rather about some future condition in which much of what is still here now will have died away. His descriptions are very accurate, for they are based on well-founded assumptions. He describes a condition of the earth several millions of years in the future when the temperature will have sunk by so and so many hundred degrees, so that certain substances – this is quite easy to calculate – will have changed. This can be calculated, and he describes how milk, for example, will not be liquid as it is today but solid, or how the albumen in eggs painted on to walls will give off so much light that one will be able to read the newspaper without the need for any other light source. He gives many other such examples. Objects which cannot withstand even a few grams of pressure will have such a strong consistency that it will be possible to suspend hundreds of kilograms from them. In short, Professor Dewar gives a marvellous account of a future state of the earth.

From the point of view of physics one cannot raise the slightest objection. But these things look entirely different to someone whose soul is filled with living thinking. If someone who has taken living thinking into his soul were to ponder the ideas put forward in the way this professor has done, he would immediately find himself confronted with something that would make him draw conclusions by a method and from a viewpoint which very much resembled the deductions and thought processes of the professor.

Let us assume that a 25-year-old human being were to be minutely observed, as can be done nowadays with the help of radiology.[13] Certain organs, let us say the stomach, are observed and the changes that take place year by year are noted; the changes in configuration are noted. This can be done in the same way as the physicist compares the sequence of changes in the earth's condition and then works out what the earth must look like after several million years. In the case of the human being you observe how, let us say, the stomach or the heart changes year by year; then, in accordance with these changes, you calculate what the human being must look like after, say, 200 years. If you do your calculations correctly the conclusions you reach will be just as well founded, only the person would have died long ago; he would no longer exist!

You see what I mean. From our own experience we know that in this case all these calculations are totally unrealistic since the human body with all those changes would no longer exist. Yet in the case of the earth such calculations are made. One fails to take into account that after two million years the earth will also have passed away and no longer exist as a physical entity, so that all these scholarly calculations about its condition have no value in reality since the reality they refer to will no longer exist.

These things are far-reaching. In the case of a human being you can equally well make the calculations backwards and, on the basis of the changes that have occurred over two years, work out what he looked like 200 years ago. Only he did not exist then! The Kant-Laplace theory has been worked out by the same method.[14] This assumes that once upon a time there was a nebulous condition which has been calculated to have existed on the basis of what exists now. The calculations are quite good and the perceptions deduced are quite correct. But the spiritual researcher finds that at the time when that nebulous condition is supposed to have existed the earth had not yet been born and the whole solar system had not yet come into being.

I wanted to use these calculations simply to show you how our whole inner life of soul must extricate itself from abstractions and immerse itself in living reality so that our inner pictures themselves can come to life. In my book *The Riddle of Man* which was published two years ago I made the distinction between real and unreal inner pictures.[15]

What matters, in brief, is that the spiritual researcher has to point out that his path is one which requires him to begin by awakening the means through which he attains knowledge and that he first has to transform his soul before he can look into the spiritual world. The results he then achieves make it obvious to others that he is not speculating about whether the soul is immortal or whether it passes through birth and death. His very path of research leads him to what is eternal in the human soul, that part which passes through births and deaths. His path of research shows him what lives eternally in the human being. He himself seeks out the object, the thing, the being. Once he has found it he can then recognize its characteristics just as one can recognize the colour of the rose.

It is because of this that it often seems as though the spiritual scientist were merely claiming such and such a thing to be the case, for by way of proof he always has to explain the path by which he reaches his conclusions. You could say he has to begin where other sciences leave off. Once this has been established there can be a real penetration into realms where it can be said that death is the starting-point, just as birth and youth is the starting-point for the earthly sciences. But it has to be made clear that the death referred to is not the death that brings to an end what can be seen externally by the senses, which is how it is usually regarded. The death in question is a part of existence, just as the forces which are brought into life by birth are a part of existence. We encounter death not only as a one-off event, for we carry the forces of death—of destruction—within us just as much as we carry within us the forces of birth, those forces given to us at birth, which are forces of construction.

To understand this fully we need to do some real research

at a boundary between natural and spiritual science. Today, though, I can only mention certain results, and of course my intention is simply to make suggestions. I would need many lectures to explain all the details of what is contained in these suggestions. Let us, then, now go to a boundary between natural and spiritual science. Although science itself has for the most part progressed beyond certain views, popular opinion still holds the views that science left behind decades ago. Therefore many still believe the human nervous system to be nothing but a tool for thinking, feeling and will, in other words for experiences of the soul. Those, however, who learn to perceive soul life by means of soul organs, spirit eyes or ears, such as I described in principle earlier on,[16] those who really discover what soul life is, know that to call the brain a tool for thinking is just like talking about walking along a muddy path and leaving footprints there which someone coming along later tries to explain. How does he explain them? By saying that down in the depths of the earth there are forces that vibrate up and down and thus produce the footprints. The footprints, however, were not caused by those forces at all, but by me when I walked there.

This is how physiologists today explain that what takes place in the brain is generated by the brain, and there is indeed something in the nervous system that corresponds to every thought and idea, every feeling. Just as my foot-prints correspond with where I have trodden, so is there something in the brain that does correspond with every impression encountered by the soul. But it is the soul that has impressed it upon the brain. The earth is just as little the organ for my treading or my footprints, it is just as little what produces them as the brain is the organ for all kinds of thought or ideation processes. I cannot walk without the ground, for I cannot walk in the air; I need the ground to walk on. And the brain is needed for the same reason, not because it produces the soul impressions but because the soul processes need the firm foundation upon which to express themselves during the period when the human being lives in a body between birth and death.

Today's sciences, which are already brilliant in themselves, will receive their ultimate explanation when this turnaround has come about, this turnaround in the way we think which I have been describing. It is a revolution more radical than was the transition to the Copernican view of the world over against the view people had cultivated prior to that, and it is also every bit as justifiable over against what has been thought until now as was the Copernican view in comparison with the views that had been held before.

There is also another aspect. As we continue along the path of soul research we find that the processes in the brain and nervous system corresponding with the life of the soul are, in fact, not constructive processes; they do not arise on account of there being constructive, thriving, flourishing processes in the nervous system such as those present in the rest of the organism. No, indeed. What the soul carries out in the nervous system is a destructive activity; while we are awake and conscious, and not asleep, it is a destructive activity. Only because our nervous system is embedded in us in such a way that it is constantly refreshed by the rest of our organism can the destructive, decomposing and demolishing activity which thinking lets loose on our nervous system be ever and again counteracted. It is a destructive activity of a quality exactly equivalent to that experienced all in one go when the human being dies, whereupon the whole of the organism disintegrates. Death lives in us constantly so long as we use our powers of thinking. In tiny amounts it is constantly within us, and the one-off event that is death is merely a summation of what is constantly at work in us. Although the dying is continuously being balanced out, this balancing is such that when the time comes death can take place as a matter of course.

We must conceive of death as a force at work in our organism just as we conceive of the forces of life. But look at science: its way of working is perfectly justified in its field, except that it seeks out only the constructive forces and remains unaware of those that are destructive. That is why it is also not possible for science to observe what continuously arises anew out of what is being destroyed. What arises anew belongs of course to the soul and spirit; it is not something bodily, for the body is constantly being destroyed. The new element is not visible for science since it can only be seen by the kind of observation which I described just now.

When we apply this observation we discover that throughout our whole life not only is every activity of our soul associated with the foundation it needs in order to function and which it even destroys, but that the totality of this activity is also a part of a spiritual world which is always around us and in which we live with the soul and spiritual part of ourselves just as much as we live in the sense-perceptible world with our physical body. So what spiritual science seeks to bring about is a genuine relationship between the human being and the spiritual world, that genuinely concrete and real spiritual world which also imbues everything physical.

It then becomes possible to observe further how the soul element that works and weaves in us and which, within the limitations I have described, brings about destruction, is in fact also a part of an overall whole. What I have termed 'soul development' pushes forward from ordinary consciousness to spiritual vision as I have written in my book *The Riddle of Man*.[17] This visionary consciousness makes it possible to attain knowledge through Imagination.[18] Imagination in this sense reveals not what is externally visible to the senses but something that belongs to the human being although it is not physically visible. This element, which is the first thing to be perceived by such newly awakened consciousness, is what I have been referring to recently as the body of formative forces.[19]

This is the supersensible body of the human being which is active throughout our whole life from birth, or one should say from conception, right up to our physical death. It is also the bearer of our memories, and as a supersensible being it is linked to a supersensible world that is external to it. Thus our physical life with its ordinary consciousness is like an island. Around this island and imbuing it lies what links our body of formative forces with the supersensible world by which this body, in its turn, is surrounded. We then see that our world of inner pictures and thoughts, just as I have described it, while being connected to our physical brain that provides it with a firm ground to stand on, is in fact carried by the body of formative forces. This is the bearer of our thinking, and our thoughts are formed within this body of formative forces, so that in the activity of thinking the human being lives within this body of formative forces.

Proceeding now to another soul experience, that of feeling, we discover that things are different. Our feelings and also our emotions and passions do not relate to our life of soul in the way our thinking does. The spiritual researcher finds that the ordinary thoughts we have are attached to the body of formative forces but that this is not the case with our feelings and emotions. Our feelings and emotions live in us in a much more subconscious way; and at the same time they are linked with something much more far-reaching than merely our life between birth and death. I do not mean that we are without thoughts in this aspect of life, for all feelings are also imbued with thoughts. But the thoughts which imbue our feelings do not usually enter our consciousness; they lie below the level of consciousness. As our feelings surge up they are interspersed with thoughts, but these thoughts are more far-reaching, and we can only find them by rising up to a higher form of consciousness than that of Imagination, namely, Inspiration, an inspired consciousness — by which I am not referring to anything connected with superstition. You can read about this in detail in my books.

By immersing ourselves in this element which, in so far as our ordinary consciousness is concerned, is asleep, just as we are asleep to ordinary sensory perceptions between falling asleep and waking up again, we shall see how it surges up just as dreams surge up while we sleep. However paradoxical this may sound, it is a fact that our feelings surge up out of the deeper part of the soul. This deeper part of the soul, which can be reached by means of Inspiration, inspired consciousness, is the part that lives on between death and a new birth; it is the part that enters into physical surroundings through our conception, or let us say our birth, and which then passes through the gate of death and goes on to lead a spiritual existence under other conditions until we are born once more. When you use the consciousness of Inspiration to examine what lives in the world of feeling, you are looking at the human being not only between birth and death but also in the period lived through between death and a further birth.

By telling you this I am not just telling you how things are, but pointing out how those forces arise in the soul which can perceive feelings, emotions and passions in a way that enables one to live within them. In a plant we see what has come into being out of the seed forces; similarly we are seeing something which does not just come into being at birth or conception but which has emerged from a spiritual world.

I am quite aware that the present-day scientific view of the world can put forward many objections to these ideas. It will be easy for those who are familiar with today's scientific views to say: 'This fellow comes along and describes in an amateurish kind of way how certain elements of his soul which he wants to grasp have emerged from a spiritual world; he describes the specific configurations and colours of his feelings in such a way that we are supposed to believe that there exists in these feelings on the one hand an indication of pre-natal existence and on the other hand something akin to the seed of a plant which contains within it what will be in the plant in the coming year. Has this fellow not heard' — these people will ask — 'of the marvellous laws of heredity which have been discovered by science? Does he not know what those who first created this branch of science discovered and put together concerning the laws of heredity?'

Of course what science points to is perfectly correct. But on the other hand it is our own forces which work to create our heredity; we work and prepare with our own forces for centuries, sending them down so that through our ancestors and parents those constellations shall be shaped that will lead to the physical result with which we clothe ourselves when we descend from the spiritual into the physical world. Those who are fully familiar with the wonderful findings of research into heredity will realize that what spiritual science has found in quite another way, by following the opposite path, the one coming from the soul, very clearly corroborates those findings, whereas what science itself has to say on these matters does not corroborate its own findings at all. This is something I can only touch on here.

Turning now to the realm of the will, we note that this is very far removed indeed from what human beings have in their ordinary consciousness. What do we know about what goes on inside us when the thought 'I want that' turns into the reaching out of our hand? The actual processes of the will are asleep in the human being. With regard to feelings and emotions we can at least state that in these we dream in ourselves. It is because the will is asleep with regard to ordinary consciousness that the question of freedom is so very fraught.

We can only reach an understanding of the processes embedded in the will if we apply the spiritual consciousness of genuine Intuition, by which I do not mean the vague and hazy kind of everyday intuitive inkling. In my writings I have referred to the three stages of consciousness: Imagination, Inspiration, Intuition. To get into the realm of the will that ought to work and live in us it first has to be hauled up out of the depths of the soul. One then also finds that this will element, too, is imbued with thought, with spiritual thoughts — not ordinary ones which are something separate.

The way we carry our will within us means that what works into it is not only what we have experienced in the spiritual world or what works into our feelings and emotions between death and a new birth. It is our experiences in former lives on earth that are at work in our will. And at the same time impulses for future lives on earth also live in what we develop and cultivate in our present will.

Genuine spiritual research sees that human life as a whole falls into two parts, those between birth and death, and the much longer ones—because the next physical existence has to be prepared over long aeons—which are experienced in the spiritual world. Human life as a whole is composed of these lives, lives on earth over and over again, and spiritual lives over and over again. This is not some fantastic notion; it is what we find if we learn to focus our spiritual eyes on all that is eternal, immortal in the human soul.

None of this excludes human freedom. If I build a house this year in which I shall live after two years, this does not detract from my freedom any more than does the way one life on earth determines the lives that will follow. It would be a misconception to put this forward as something that infringes the idea of human freedom.

So, with spiritual research one gradually begins to reach spiritual facts when one takes death as the starting-point. All kinds of observations can be made when death is taken as the foundation on which spiritual research begins in the same way as birth and burgeoning life is the foundation for physical research. I shall mention a few examples, as I don't want to go round and round without being specific but would prefer to give some concrete results of anthroposophical spiritual research. In ordinary spiritual life we can distinguish between violent death due to external causes, and death from within, brought on perhaps by an illness or old age. So there are various kinds of death, and when spiritual research looks at the concrete nature of death we find the following.

Let us take the example of a violent death, whether it is brought about by an accident or some other cause. Such a death is an event that brings the present life to an end. The development of one's spiritual awareness of the spiritual world after death depends just as much on this one-off event of death as the development of a basis for our consciousness in life — in the way I have described it — depends on the basis of forces which are given us at birth. After death the kind of consciousness we develop is different. Here on earth our consciousness rests on the foundation of our nervous system in the same way as I stand or walk on the ground. Our consciousness in the spiritual world after death is different, but it is definitely a consciousness. When someone dies a violent death this is not only something that affects his thinking. Ordinary consciousness ceases with death, of course, but another kind of consciousness begins, and this affects the person's will, of which we have seen that it goes over into subsequent lives on earth. The spiritual researcher possesses the means by which he can investigate what can come up in an earthly life if the previous life ended in violent death.

Obviously many people will say that to speak about such things is foolish, childish or fantastical. But the results I am talking about are every bit as reliable scientifically — for I only quote reliable results — as are those of the physical sciences. When a violent death intervenes in someone's life this has consequences for the next life on earth by bringing it about that at a specific point in that life a change of direction occurs. Research into the life of the soul is going on even now, but on the whole this investigates only the most external aspects. A moment can arrive in a person's life when the whole course of his destiny changes and he steps out on new paths as though inwardly challenged to do so. Such things are termed 'conversions' in America because people like to give things a name. But it is not necessarily always a matter of religion. A person can be forced into a new direction of life, a permanent change in the direction in which his will takes him. A radical change like this in the direction of one's will originates in the violent end of the previous life. How frequently the type of death is of importance especially in the middle of the subsequent life is made obvious to concrete research. If death comes about naturally through sickness or old age, then it has much more importance for the life between death and the next birth than it has for the next earthly life.

I wanted to mention these examples to show you that rather than going round and round without being specific one can indeed gain quite specific insights about details that occur in the context of a lifetime. Even for those who are already convinced that the soul is immortal, spiritual research can make them aware that one need not speak only in general terms about this, for understanding what is eternal in the human soul leads to human life itself becoming comprehensible. All the remarkable processes one observes if one has a sense for the soul element in life, for the way the life of soul progresses in the human being, all those wonderful events enter into the picture if one knows that this has to do with repeated lives on earth and repeated lives in the spiritual world.

Let me add in parenthesis: In the spiritual world the human being relates to spiritual beings—not only fellow human beings who have been close to him in his destiny and who have also passed through the gate of death but also other spiritual beings—in the same way as he relates here on earth to the three earthly kingdoms, the plant, the mineral and the animal kingdom. The spiritual researcher speaks of specific individual spirits, specific individual spiritual beings, indeed of a spiritual world of actual individual beings just as here on earth we speak of individual plant and animal beings and also human beings as they are as physical beings between birth and death.

What happens when such spiritual knowledge enters your soul in a certain specific way is something that affects you very profoundly. From what I have said you will have seen that one can gain knowledge about the spiritual world. Such knowledge is profoundly important for the human soul; in fact, in a way it changes the human soul into something else. It takes hold of your life of soul regardless of whether you are a spiritual researcher yourself or whether you have only heard and understood and absorbed what a spiritual researcher has told you. It does not matter whether you have discovered it yourself so long as you comprehend it. And you can comprehend all of it so long as you enter deeply enough into it. It is a matter of having taken it into yourself. Then, once you have grasped the whole inner essence of it, something will enter your soul which will make you realize that this is more significant than anything else that has ever happened in your life.

You may have had difficult or sad experiences that have affected you deeply, or joyful ones, uplifting ones, for if you are a spiritual researcher or someone who sees into the spirit you need not be unreceptive to such experiences but can enter into them with as much feeling as anyone who is not yet a spiritual researcher. But when you have grasped the whole inner essence of what spiritual knowledge gives your soul and can say what it is that this spiritual knowledge gives to your soul, when you can fully realize what your soul has become through this spiritual knowledge, then this event will become more significant than every other experience of destiny that has come upon you. The other experiences do not grow smaller, but this one grows larger. Spiritual knowledge then enters in through the life of your soul as a part of your destiny. When spiritual knowledge enters in through the life of your soul you begin to comprehend human destiny itself; from that moment onwards a light shines on to human destiny and clarifies it.

From that moment onwards you realize that having this experience of destiny in such a purely spiritual way enables you to explain how destiny has positioned you in life, how one's destiny hangs on threads that have been spun out from former lives on earth as well as lives between death and a new birth, threads that then spin on from this life into the one that follows. You realize that ordinary consciousness merely dreams its way through destiny; ordinary consciousness merely accepts destiny without understanding it, just as one accepts dreams. Spiritual consciousness, in which we wake up as we wake up from dreams into ordinary consciousness, gains us a new relationship to destiny. We recognize destiny as that which works with us on our overall life, the life that proceeds on and on through births and deaths.

This must not be understood in a superficial way by simply saying that one has brought one's misfortune on oneself. To do this would be to misunderstand spiritual research, indeed it would be to cast slanderous aspersions on it. (And anyway, a misfortune need not necessarily have its cause in one's former life. It may have happened spontaneously, in which case there would be consequences in the next life and in the whole of the life between the two lives on earth, for it is often to be seen that from misfortune, and also suffering and pain, there grows a different kind of consciousness in the spiritual world.) What happens through this new spiritual knowledge is that meaning enters our whole life, understanding for our destiny which we normally dream our way through but which we now come to comprehend.

Something comes to the fore especially when we focus on this spiritual knowledge, and that is that we cannot simply go on saying: Well, so after death the soul enters into another life, but let's wait until that happens; let's live life now as it is lived in the physical body and wait until later to see what happens after death. This whole question is a matter of consciousness.

Of course what happens after death is in some way connected with the life we live here in our physical body. Here through our body we have the consciousness of the normal waking state. After death, though, we have a consciousness that is not spatial and founded on our nervous system but temporal and built on looking backwards. We have in our nervous system the counterbalance and counterstroke for our ordinary consciousness between birth and death, whereas the foundation for our consciousness in the spiritual world between death and a new birth is formed by what is already in our consciousness here. Just as we are here surrounded by the world, so, once we have died, does our life present itself before us as an important organ. Therefore much depends on the consciousness we have while we are in our physical body, since this reaches out into the consciousness that comes to meet us after death. For example, as often happens with present-day habits of thought a person may be exclusively concerned with physical thoughts and ideas arising through the senses. In his memories and in everything taking place in his soul such a person has in his consciousness only ideas based on ordinary life. This person, too, is building up the world that will surround him after death. We build up our environment in accordance with what we are inwardly. Just as someone born in Europe cannot see himself surrounded by America, just as we receive our environment from the surroundings we are born into, so do we in some way determine the environment, the place where we exist, through what we have created whilst in our body.

Take an extreme case which, however, is not very likely to occur. Think of a person who resists all supersensible ideas, someone who has become an atheist and has not gained even from religion the slightest feeling that he might want to take an interest in such things. (I know that I am speaking in paradoxes, but what I am saying has a good foundation in spiritual science.) Such a person is condemning himself to remain in the sphere of the earth, to remain here with his consciousness, whereas someone who has taken in spiritual ideas can enter into a spiritual environment. The person who has ideas based solely on the senses condemns himself to remain in the sense-perceptible environment.

We can work in a beneficial way when we are in our physical body in the physical world, for here our physical body acts as a protective cloak. But if we remain present in the physical world after death we work in a detrimental way. When our consciousness harbours physical ideas and inner pictures after death we become destroyers. I have already pointed out, in connection with the laws of heredity, how the human being's forces intervene in the physical world even when he is in the spiritual world. Those who cultivate only a physical consciousness and thus condemn themselves to remaining in the physical world become the focus for destructive forces that interfere in what happens in people's lives and in the world at large.

So long as we are in our body that body remains a protection even if we have nothing but materialistic thoughts to do with sense-perceptible things. In fact our body is a far greater protection than we imagine. It is most strange, but someone who can look into the whole context of the spiritual world comes to be quite sure about a certain fact. Since we are unable in ordinary consciousness to take in living concepts but can only absorb dead ones which hold us back from entering into our spiritual surroundings, it is a fact that if we were not separated from our environment by our senses, if our senses did not keep things away from us, if we could make our thoughts and ideas effective rather than just having them within us once things have passed through our senses, then already here in the physical world our life of thoughts would have a deathly, paralysing effect. This is because such thoughts and ideas are in a certain way destructive for everything that is grasped by them. It is solely because they are retained within us that these thoughts and ideas are not destructive. They only bring about destruction when they come to expression in machines, in tools which are something dead that has been removed from living nature. Although this is just a picture it nevertheless corresponds to a reality.

So, when a human being enters into the spiritual world with nothing but physical thoughts and ideas he becomes a focus of destruction. I have given this one example in place of many which could show us that, no, we cannot wait to see what will happen. It is up to us in our own being to develop thoughts and ideas which are either only materialistic or which are supersensible, thus preparing in the one way or the other way for the life to come. That life will of course be entirely different, but it does evolve out of the life we lead here. This is the essential fact that we must realize.

A good many things can crop up for us out of spiritual science that are different from what we expected. I must therefore conclude with a few more remarks.

One might easily presume that to be someone who can enter into the spiritual world one must of necessity become a spiritual researcher. This is not necessary, although I have written a great deal in my book *How to Know Higher Worlds* about what the soul must do in order to enter there. Anyone can do this to some extent today, but not everyone needs to do so. What you develop in your soul is an entirely inner affair; but what it leads to is that the truths being researched can be formulated into concepts, so that you can clothe in thoughts and ideas — like those I have put forward today — what a spiritual researcher tells you. It is something that can be communicated. One of the laws of spiritual research is that it does not matter whether you have found these things out through your own research or whether you have been informed about them by a reliable source. It is not a matter of finding these things out yourself, for the important thing is that you have them and develop them within yourself.

It is, then, a misunderstanding to assume that everyone must become a spiritual researcher. But nowadays someone who is a spiritual researcher will have the need, as I had the need, to give an account of the path he has followed for his research. This is not only because anyone today can to some extent tread the described path without coming to any harm but also because anyone has the right to ask: 'What did you do to arrive at these results?' That is why I have described these things. I also believe that those who do not want to become spiritual researchers do nevertheless want to find out how a spiritual researcher arrives at his findings, for these findings are what all those need who, in keeping with the stage human evolution has now reached, want to lay foundations for the life that must develop in human souls.

The age is now over in which the discoveries of spiritual research and what they brought about in human soul development were very much kept away from the public eye. In olden times it was strictly forbidden to pass on what was hidden, and even today those who know about these secrets of life — and there are not a few such individuals — shrink from divulging them. The implication is that if you have received such things from someone else who is a teacher, you will do well not to pass them on under any circumstances! It is advisable to pass on only one's own discoveries, and it is these that can and indeed must be placed in the service of the rest of humanity.

Even the few brief hints I have given today will show what spiritual research can mean for the individual person. But it is not only for individuals that such research is important, and in order to show very briefly why this is I want to conclude by saying a few words about something of which very little account is taken nowadays.

Let me draw your attention to a remarkable phenomenon. The second half of the nineteenth century saw the spectacular rise of a particular scientific trend, namely, the explanation of living nature linked with the name of Darwin.[20] Enthusiastic scholarly researchers and their enthusiastic pupils carried this trend forward throughout the latter decades of the nineteenth century. I may even here have mentioned the extraordinary development to which this led. As early as the 1860s a gigantic movement came into being under the leadership of Haeckel,[21] a movement that strove to throw aside everything that was old and redesign the whole view of the world to fit in with Darwin's concepts. Even today there are still those who stress how grand and important it would be if instead of having a wisdom-filled guidance for the universe we could have explained on the basis of Darwinism how everything has come into being.

In 1869 Eduard von Hartmann came forward with his *Philosophy of the Unconscious*,[22] turning against Darwinism, which saw the world purely in external terms, and pointing to the need for inner forces, though he did this in an inadequate, merely philosophical manner—having no spiritual research to go on. Those whose enthusiasm focused on Darwinism were of course prepared to call this philosopher a dilettante to whom it was not necessary to listen. Writings were published mocking the dilettante Eduard von Hartmann and stating that there was no call for a genuine scientist to take note of such views.

An anonymous paper appeared with a brilliant refutation of Hartmann's thoughts.[23] The scientists and those who thought as they did were in full agreement with this paper, for it completely refuted Eduard von Hartmann. Everything that could be brought forward in a scholarly manner on the basis of science was indeed brought forward in this paper written by an anonymous author against Hartmann—in rather the same way as objections are put forward today against spiritual research. This paper was much applauded. Haeckel intoned: 'Here is a genuine scientist writing to refute that dilettante Hartmann; here we see what a real scientist can do; indeed I could not have written anything better myself; let him come forward and we will accept him as one of our own.'[24] In short, the scientists made a good deal of propaganda about this paper which suited them so well, and it was soon out of print. A second edition was needed, and then the author himself came forward: he was Eduard von Hartmann!

Here was someone who taught the world an important lesson. Any spiritual researcher today who comes up against what is written against spiritual research could produce all of it off the top of his own head with ease, just as Eduard von Hartmann was himself quite capable of presenting everything the scientists had to say against him — and did so.

But all this is merely an introduction to what I really want say, which is this: Oscar Hertwig is one of Haeckel's most important pupils and has himself trodden the assiduous and honest and great path of scientific research.[25] Last year he brought out a very fine book, *Das Werden der Organismen. Eine Widerlegung von Darwin's Zufallstheorie* (The evolution of organisms. A refutation of Darwin's theory of chance). In this book he points to matters like those also brought up by Eduard von Hartmann. This is an almost unique case of the very next generation, the one which grew up under the direct influence of the master, turning its back on something that had been expected to provide the basis for a whole world view and even give answers regarding the spiritual world. A good Darwinist refuting Darwinism! In fact, he goes even further, and this is what I want to point to at the end of this lecture.

At the end of his excellent and fine book Oscar Hertwig states that a world view of the kind put forward by Darwin is more than merely a theoretical construct, for it affects the whole of people's lives right down into what they do, want, feel and think. He says:

Interpretations of Darwin's theory, which is so ambiguous owing to its very vagueness, have made it applicable in a great variety of ways to other realms of economic, social and political life. As though from a Delphic oracle it has been possible to take whatever one wanted and make use of it with reference to social, political, health, medical and other questions by using the science of a Darwinistically reworked biology with its unalterable laws to back up one's claims. If, however, these presumed laws are in fact no such thing, does this not mean that there could be social dangers in applying them so variously to other fields? Do not believe that human society can spend half a century using such phrases as 'the inexorable struggle for existence', 'the survival of the fittest, of the most useful, of the most suitable', 'perfection through selective breeding' and so on as freely as eating its daily bread without finding its ideas becoming more deeply and more persistently influenced by them! It would not be hard to find many phenomena to prove that this is happening, and this is the very reason why judgement as to whether Darwinism is true or erroneous has implications far beyond the scope of the biological sciences.[26]

Life is now showing us on every side what is revealed by such a theory. And the same question, also impinging on life, arises from the angle of spiritual science. We are living in a time of sorrow, one that is tragic for humanity. It is a time that has surely evolved out of human beings' inner pictures and ideas. Those of us who look at the links between such things from the point of view of spiritual science know what it is that connects the events now confronting us externally with all the tragedy we are experiencing. We are experiencing a great deal, and people imagine they know what is going on, they imagine they can fully comprehend this reality with their concepts; but they cannot. And being unable to comprehend the events fully on the basis of their concepts they blunder into them only to discover the chaos that ensues and with which we are now surrounded.

Spiritual science arises out of an inner necessity; but this is not the only reason, for it would certainly have arisen anyway out of inner necessity even if external events had not now pointed the way like a mighty and powerful sign. Although the traditional view of the world is fine as regards today's scientific attitude, the fact is that this view will never be able to come to grips with social, legal or political matters in the world. In fact, if I may put it like this, people fail to cope with reality and it is this that brings in a new angle which points towards spiritual science with powerful signs, a spiritual science which seeks for concepts that are in tune with reality, concepts drawn from this very reality that will therefore also be capable of supporting the world socially and indeed politically.

However strongly we imagine we shall be capable of extricating ourselves from the chaos on the basis of current concepts which take no note of spiritual science, we shall be unable to do so, for it is spirit that holds sway in the real world. And because human actions influence the realities of social and political life, people need to arrive at fruitful concepts, they need thoughts, feelings and will impulses that have been drawn down out of the spirit. Politics and the social sciences will in future need something for which only spiritual science can provide the basis. This is something that is of outstanding importance for contemporary history.

I myself can only make a few isolated suggestions in this lecture which has already become quite long enough. What

I want to point out is that the spiritual science coming into being today in an orderly and systematic way is something which the best individuals wish to bring about. If the choice were mine I would attach one particular name to this spiritual science. For 30 years or more I have been working to give ever greater clarity to the ideas which Goethe derived from reality in his marvellous theory of metamorphosis,[27] in which he strove to bring alive what would otherwise have been dead concepts. In his day only a beginning could be made. But if we regard Goethe as belonging not only historically to his own time but also to the present day we find that especially his theory of metamorphosis brings into being living concepts which can then find their way into spiritual science.

I would love to give the name 'Goetheanism' to what I mean by 'spiritual research', for the latter rests on the healthy foundation of a way of looking at reality which would have met with Goethe's approval. And I would greatly prefer to give the name 'Goetheanum' to the building at Dornach[28] which is devoted to that spiritual research and through which that research has become more known than would perhaps otherwise have been the case, for to call the building 'the Goetheanum' would be to show that the spiritual research carried out today stands firmly and healthily within the process of human evolution.

Of course many people today still believe that they are adhering to Goethe's view of the world when they state that Goethe was the one who recognized nature as the highest and who even saw how the spirit emerges from nature. It was indeed Goethe who, as a very young man, said, 'She thought and she ponders constantly,'[29] nature ponders constantly, though not as a human being does but as nature does. Well, even as spiritual researchers we can certainly be in agreement with a type of naturalism that regards nature as being filled with spirit in the way Goethe did. And the reply we can give to those who always believe that one should come to a halt at the boundaries of knowledge, since there can be no path beyond, can be framed in Goethe's own words. So let me conclude by quoting the words Goethe uttered about another well-deserving researcher who represented Kant's later views:

'Into the core of Nature
No earthly mind can enter.
Happy the mortal creature
To whom she shows no more
Than the outer rind.'[30]

Goethe then countered these words with others, which show how well he knew that the individual who awakens the spirit within himself will find the spirit in the world as well, and also himself as a spirit therein:

'Into the core of Nature
No earthly mind can enter.
Happy the mortal creature
To whom she shows no more
Than the outer rind,'
For sixty years I've heard your sort announce.
It makes me swear, though quietly.
Nature has neither core
Nor outer rind,
Being all things at once.
It's yourself you should scrutinize to see
Whether you're centre or periphery.[31]

Spiritual science wants to lead human beings to examine seriously whether they are either centre or periphery. They are centre if they fully comprehend their whole reality. If they comprehend themselves as centre they can press onwards to the spirit in nature. And when that happens something will enter into human evolution with regard to spiritual research which will resemble what had to happen when Copernicus moved from the visible to the invisible when pointing to something visible.

In order to reach the supersensible realm, human beings will have to take the trouble to comprehend the super-sensible within themselves. To do this one need not become a spiritual researcher; but one must indeed sweep away all those prejudices that lay siege to the soul when one endeavours to comprehend what is meant by spiritual research in the Goethean sense.

These are the few suggestions I wanted to make today. In fact, suggestions are all one can voice, for if I wanted to explain all this in every detail I would have to give a great many lectures. I believe that these few explanations will suffice to show that something is waiting to be won from the process of human evolution, something that when found will awaken the human soul to abundant life. No one need fear that this will cause the soul to wither or that other things might die away, not even their religious life. It is as Goethe said:

If science and art are yours
Then religion is yours too.
But if you lack either of these
Then may you at least have religion![32]

So let us allow ourselves to say something that is in keeping with today's way of thinking: If you find the way to the paths of spiritual science you will also discover true re-ligious life; but if you do not find the way to paths of spiritual science, then it must be feared that you are likely to lose also the religious path that is so much needed for the future of humanity.

2. The Mystery of the Double. Geographic Medicine

You will have realized that something very important for an understanding of spiritual knowledge in connection with human life was said at yesterday's public lecture.[1] I suggested that there are people nowadays who prefer, while they are on the physical plane, to take in only ideas that derive from the sense-perceptible world, ideas that can be won only by an intellect that relates solely to the sense-perceptible world while rejecting anything else. I said that after their death such people are bound to an environment that still retains leanings towards the earthly, physical region in which we live between birth and death. In the way they live in the physical body such people condemn themselves to a long sojourn in the earthly, physical world even after they have died, thus causing destructive forces to be created within this physical world.

This touches on profound and important esoteric matters that have to do with human life, esoteric matters that have been painstakingly guarded for centuries, indeed millennia, by certain secret societies. These societies have maintained — by what right we shall not investigate just now — that human beings are too immature to receive such truths or secrets and that revealing them would give rise to much bewilderment. Today we shall not go into the right by which such profoundly incisive truths that are so important for human life have been withheld and only cultivated within the closed circle of esoteric schools.[2] But what has to be said is that the time has now come when humanity at large can, indeed must, no longer be left in ignorance of certain secrets about the supersensible world such as those I mentioned yesterday.

Within certain bounds it was justified in former times, when circumstances were different, to keep such esoteric matters hidden, but now this is no longer the case. As we know, we are now living in the fifth post-Atlantean epoch.[3] It is a time when the conditions pertaining to human life are such that to go through the gate of death would entail becoming a destroyer unless one had spent this life searching increasingly for inner pictures, concepts and ideas about supersensible matters. So we can no longer agree with those who maintain that we might as well wait and see what will happen when we die. We cannot do this because it is necessary for us to know now — between our birth and our death — about certain matters concerning the spiritual world, as I pointed out yesterday, in order to be in possession of these inner pictures and ideas when we step through the gate of death.

This was not the same in earlier periods of human evolution. As you know, up to the sixteenth century, when the Copernican view was presented, people had quite different beliefs about the structure of the universe. Obviously it was necessary for human progress, and to enable human freedom to enter into the evolution of humanity, that the Copernican view of the world should make its appearance on the scene, just as it is now necessary for spiritual science to appear. Nevertheless, the physical view of the world which people had before the arrival of Copernicanism — call it wrong, if you wish — that view of a physical world in which the earth stood still while the sun and the stars circled round its skies, and where beyond those skies there was a spiritual sphere where spiritual beings lived, that was a view which human beings could still take with them through the gate of death without being held back in the earthly sphere once they had died. It was a view of the world which did not cause them to become destroyers in the earthly sphere once they had passed through the gate of death. But when Copernicanism burst upon the scene it brought a view of the whole universe spread out in space ruled only by spatial laws; and it was when Copernicanism showed the earth circling round the sun that this view bound human beings to physical, sense-perceptible existence and prevented them from rising up into the spiritual world in the appropriate way after death.

This drawback of the Copernican world view has to be acknowledged today despite the fact that preparations were made for centuries to bring this wonderful advancement to human souls. Both sides are equally justified. The one side shows how clever it is—though in the interim the opinion that the Copernican world view is the only satisfying one now shows this cleverness up to be somewhat philistine. Nevertheless, it is still clever, but the other side, that this Copernican world view ties human beings to the earth after they have died if they have not gained a spiritual view, is regarded by people today as foolishness; yet it is the truth. You know even from the Bible that some things which human beings call foolishness are in fact wisdom to the gods.[4]

When a human being steps through the gate of death his consciousness changes. So it would be wrong to believe that you are unconscious after death. Yet this strange idea is fairly widespread even in circles that call themselves 'theosophical'. It is nonsense, however, for consciousness then becomes, on the contrary, much mightier, much more intensive; but it is different. Even as far as our ordinary ideas about the physical world go it has to be said that our conscious ideas after death are different.

Most importantly, it is after death that people unite with those with whom they have been karmically linked in life. It can happen that someone who has died encounters many human souls in the spiritual world between death and a new birth. He passes through these souls — for here things are permeable, not impermeable — or moves past them, but as far as he is concerned they are not there. Those who *are* there for him are the ones with whom he is karmically linked in some way.

To grow together more and more into a general world coherence, also after death, is something we have to work for through our life here on earth. Founding societies that are built purely on spirit is therefore one of our tasks now and in the future. Why do we endeavour to found societies such as the Anthroposophical Society? Why do we seek to unite people under the heading of such ideas? We do it so as to create karmic links between individuals who are to find one another in the spiritual world, which is something they could not do if they were to go around here all alone. By enabling people to share spiritual knowledge and spiritual wisdom amongst each other we create immense opportunities for their life in the spiritual world, and this in turn works back to the physical, sense-perceptible world which is constantly influenced by the spiritual world. In fact, what we have here are only the effects, for even when we are here on the physical plane the causes happen over there in the spiritual world.

There is so much propaganda about such things today

when societies are set up for all kinds of reasons, and often with the greatest of enthusiasm, but few are devoted to spiritual matters. People think that some of these societies will gradually change the world into an earthly paradise. Well, there were plenty of them three years ago before this war broke out and a good many people were working towards transforming Europe into just such an earthly paradise. But our situation now does not hold out much hope that events can be directed in the way people had hoped.

In other ways, though, collaboration of the physical with the spiritual world is more complicated. Nevertheless, it has to be said that if societies are founded in the light of spiritual science, this means that through them people collaborate not only with the world of effects but also with the world of the causes that underlie the world of effects. We must imbue ourselves with this feeling entirely if we are to understand rightly the immeasurable and profound significance of what is achieved through living together in spiritual collaboration now and in the future of humanity.

This is not something that can be gained on the basis of any kind of clubby fellowship, for it is a sacred task laid upon present and future humanity by the divine spiritual beings who govern the world. People will be unable to avoid taking in at least some inner conceptions about the supersensible world because such conceptions will less and less be forthcoming from the sense-perceptible world. By its very progress, science will increasingly drive conceptions about the supersensible world out of the world of the senses. If human beings failed to take in any supersensible, spiritual concepts, this would eventually exclude them entirely from the spiritual world; they would be con-demning themselves to becoming after death totally bound up with the physical earth alone, and with what the physical earth will one day become.

Since the physical earth will become a corpse in the future, human beings would thus be facing the frightful prospect of condemning themselves to inhabiting a corpse in the guise of its soul if they failed to decide that they must learn how to live in the spiritual world and take root there. A most important task has thus indeed been set for the cultivation of spiritual science. Once every day we should fill our soul with this sacred thought so as never again to lose our enthusiasm for this matter of spiritual science.

All those inner conceptions which can multiply more and more if we join in with the many concepts about the spiritual world which have already come from that world into our spiritual stream, all these conceptions that are coming to us enable us to free ourselves from being bound to the earth, to what is destructive in the earthly realm, so that we can derive our work from another direction. So we do remain linked with the souls we have left behind on the earth and with those with whom we are karmically connected, and also with the earth, but from the direction of other realms. We are in fact more intensively linked with the souls left behind on the earth when our links with them derive from higher spiritual realms and when we are not condemned by a purely materialistic way of life to haunt the earth like ghosts without being linked through love with anything on it but are turned instead into focuses of destruction.

We know how from childhood onwards we develop our consciousness here on earth and how it grows and thrives; there is no need to describe this here. But after death quite other processes are at work by which we gradually achieve the consciousness we need for our life between death and a new birth. Here on the earth we go about, learn things and have experiences; but this is not what happens after death. There is no longer any need for this then.

What must then happen is that we have to detach from ourselves something immensely intensive which is tied up with us once we have left our physical body behind. Having passed through the gate of death we come into a relationship with the spiritual world described here by spiritual science; we grow together with it. We have described this as the world of the higher hierarchies, the Angeloi, Archangeloi, Archai, the Exusiai, Dynamis, Kyriotetes and so on, the world of the higher hierarchies together with their deeds and experiences.[5] Here on earth the world is outside us; the world of the mineral, plant and animal kingdoms is in our environment. But when we have passed through the gate of death the spiritual beings we list as the higher hierarchies, and indeed their very worlds, are within us. We are bound up with them and can at first not distinguish ourselves from them; we live in them and they imbue us entirely. This is a difficult concept to come to grips with, but we have to make ourselves familiar with it. Here we are outside the world; there we are within the world. Our own being spreads out all over the whole world; but we cannot distinguish ourselves from it. After death we are as though stuffed full of the beings of the higher hierarchies and with whatever it is that they are doing. Most importantly, what we have to do is detach the more lofty hierarchies from the one that is closest to us, the hierarchy of Angeloi, Archangeloi and Archai which fills us entirely.

I have described in other lectures and contexts how our I-consciousness grows and matures in a proper way. Over there we cannot achieve a proper I-consciousness if we do not have the strength to distinguish: What is in me? Is it an

Angelos? Is it one of the Elohim? What is a being from the hierarchy of the Angeloi, what is a being from the hierarchy of the Exusiai, the Spirits of Form? Over there we have to learn to distinguish and we have to have the strength to detach what we want to perceive from what is bound up with us; otherwise it is in us and not there outside us. Here on earth we have to link up with what is outside us and look at it; over there we have to detach it from ourselves in order to be linked with it.

At the stage the world has now reached in human evolution we must acquire spiritual concepts if we want to detach from ourselves something we would otherwise carry within us only as though asleep. People find these spiritual concepts awkward because they have to make some effort, more effort than would be necessary for ordinary concepts. But if they acquire them, then, after death these concepts develop tremendous power, and it is this power alone that gives us the ability to recognize and comprehend the spiritual world. This is exceedingly important. People today feel uncomfortable if they have to acquire spiritual concepts. They like going to meetings where they are shown lantern slides or similar things and therefore do not have to think in a supersensible way; they like to see things in front of them, or at least hear lectures that tell them only about what they anyway always have before their eyes. People today shy away from making an effort to ascend to concepts that are more difficult here because they have no outer object since their objects are the facts that relate to the supersensible world. Over there, however, these concepts are the forces which actually bring the reality of the world to us.

Through spiritual ideas and concepts we gain the wisdom we need in order to have light over there where otherwise everything will be in darkness. What we attain here in the way of wisdom is light, spiritual light, over there. Wisdom is spiritual light. We need wisdom in order not to find ourselves in darkness over there. Not to acquire spiritual concepts is the best way of having no light over there. And when one has no light one moves away again from the sphere into which one ought to be casting light; one drifts back to earth and wanders about there as a focus of destruction. At most one might be used from time to time by a black magician in order to provide inspiration for certain quite specific functions, but also for destructive activities on the earth.

Wisdom, then, is something we need so that we can have light after death. But there is something else we need after death as well. The ability to detach the beings of the spiritual world in order to be able to confront them is not the only thing we need, for we also have to have the faculty of love. If we did not have this we would be unable to develop a proper relationship with the beings whom wisdom enables us to perceive. We need the faculty of love. However, the love engendered here on the earth is for the most part dependent on our physical body. This love is a feeling and it depends on the rhythm of breathing here in the physical world. It is not the kind of love that we can take with us into the spiritual world. It would be a complete illusion to believe that we can take this love over with us into the spiritual world, especially the kind of love we develop here at this particular time. What we do take over into the spiritual world is all the power of the love we acquire here in the physical world through perceiving this world with our senses, through living with this physical world.

This love is fired in us by the understanding we can

develop for the physical world as we live here in it. If we take into our feeling life specifically those experiences we can have in viewing the world by means of modern science, this leads to love developing for when we are over on the other side.

Love, however, is something that can be either high or low depending on the realm in which it unfolds. If you pass through the gate of death and then have to remain in the earth realm as a focus of destruction, well, this is also due to having developed great love. The fact that you have to remain like this is a consequence of your having been bound up with purely naturalistic concepts, but then you employ this love for works of destruction; you love the work of destruction and are condemned to observe yourself loving the work of destruction.

Love, then, is noble if you can rise up to higher worlds and love what you gain through spiritual concepts. We must on no account forget this: Love is lowly when it works in a lowly sphere, and it is noble and high and spiritual when it works in a higher, a spiritual sphere. This is the essential point to be remembered. If you remain unaware of this you will be unable to discern things in the right way.

People today must become familiar with ideas like these pertaining to the human being's life after death. For humanity as it is today, and especially as it will be in the near future, it is no longer sufficient for people to be told by preachers that they should believe something or other and that they must prepare for eternal life if these preachers are incapable of describing what it looks like in the world human beings go to after passing through the gate of death. In former times when scientific, naturalistic concepts did not yet exist, and because people had not yet become infected with the merely material interests which have gained so much ground since the sixteenth century, it was in order for preachers to talk about the supersensible world in the way the various religious denominations still want to talk today. But this is not in order now. In deep compassion for humanity it unfortunately has to be said that people today often become ensnared for the very reason that they want to promote their own eternal bliss in an egoistic way via the religious denominations. By this very means they become excessively ensnared in the physical, sense-perceptible natural world, thus blocking their own ascent once they have passed through the gate of death.

This is yet another reason why it is necessary to empha-size profoundly how important it is for humanity to occupy itself with spiritual science in the present time and in the future, for those who are unable to form ideas about the life after death deserve the utmost commiseration. One of many reasons for the need to try and spread the word about spiritual science is that it must be done out of deepest sympathy for people because it is so lamentable if, from lack of understanding, they continue to resist making any approach to the ideas of spiritual science.

The spiritual world is everywhere, and we must be quite clear about this. Only think of the world in which the dead are with the dead, that supersensible world with the threads which link the dead with the living who have been left behind, and the threads which link the dead with the higher hierarchies; all this belongs to the world in which we find ourselves. As truly as the air is all around us, just as truly is that world always around us too. We are not at all separated off from that world, for it is only different states of consciousness that separate us from the world we move in after death. This must be clearly emphasized, for even within our circles not all our friends are really clear about the fact that the dead person finds the living person once more, in all his fullness, and that we are only separated so long as the one here is in a physical body and the other there without a physical body. All these forces which bring us close to the dead have to be attained by means of our letting go of them. If we do not do this, we have them within us and thus cannot perceive them. Then we must also attain the ability to bring across into the proper sphere the power of love which develops through the naturalistic ideas that are here, for otherwise this power will become an evil power for us over there. That love in particular which develops through naturalistic ideas could otherwise become an evil power. A power or force as such is neither good nor evil; it can be one or the other, depending on which sphere it appears in.

Just as we are linked with that supersensible world where the dead are, so does the supersensible world also reach out into the physical, sense-perceptible world in another way as well. The cosmos is indeed complicated, and we can only come to grasp it slowly and gradually. But we must have the will to grasp it.

The spiritual world reaches out into our world. Everything is interspersed with the spiritual world. In everything that is sense-perceptible there is also something that is not sense-perceptible. Human beings ought to be especially interested in that part of the supersensible which has to do with their own sense-perceptible nature. So please consider what I am going to say carefully, for it is an extremely important image.

We human beings are structured according to body, soul and spirit, but this does not account for our whole being by a long way. Our body, our soul and our spirit are what we are immediately concerned with as belonging to our consciousness. But this is by a long way not all that our existence involves. What I now want to describe is connected with certain secrets of human evolution, of human nature, and these, too, must now become known, and ever better known.

When a human being enters earthly existence through birth he gains on the one hand the possibility of giving a means of existence to his soul through his physical body. Please take note of this. But on the other hand a person does not know his physical body at all well. What an extraordinary number of things go on in our body of which we know nothing! Then gradually we do begin to learn through anatomy and physiology something of what goes on there, although this is not at all a particularly adequate way of learning these things. If we had to wait before taking any nourishment until we understood about the digestive processes, well, it is pointless even to mention that we would starve; for it is unthinkable that we can know what our organs have to do in order to process our food for our organism.

So, we arrive in this world with the garment of our organism without being able to reach down into it with our soul to any great extent. Instead, shortly before we are born, not very long before we are born, there is also an opportunity for another spiritual being, apart from our soul, to take possession of our body, namely, of the subconscious part of our body. This is a fact. Shortly before we are born another being indwells us; in the terminology we use today we would call this an ahrimanic being. It is just as much in us as is our own soul.

These beings lead their lives by making use of human beings to enable them to inhabit the sphere in which they wish to dwell. They have an exceptionally high degree of intelligence and a very significantly developed will, but no qualities of soul, nothing like what we would call the human qualities of soul and heart and mind. So we proceed through our life while having our soul and also a double who is far cleverer, far cleverer than we are, very intelligent, but with a mephistophelian intelligence, an ahrimanic intelligence, and in addition also an ahrimanic will, a very strong will, a will that is much more akin to the forces of nature than it is to our human will which is ruled by our heart and mind.

In the nineteenth century science discovered that our nervous system is interspersed with forces of electricity. Science was quite right. But the scientists are wrong if they believe that the nervous force which belongs to us and which provides the foundation for our inner world of pictures and thinking has anything to do with the electric currents that course along our nerves. Those electric currents are the forces that are introduced into our being by the being I have just been describing. They do not belong to our being at all. There are electrical currents in us, but they are of a purely ahrimanic nature.

These beings of high intelligence, of a purely mephistophelian intelligence, and of a will more akin to nature than can be said of our human will, these beings have decided out of their own will that they do not want to live in the world to which they were assigned by the wise gods of the upper hierarchies. They want to conquer the earth, so they need bodies. Having no bodies of their own they use as much of human bodies as they can since the human soul cannot quite fill out the human body.

While a human body is developing, these beings can slip into it at a specific point before birth, and thereafter they accompany us beneath the threshold of our consciousness.

But there is one aspect of human life which they cannot stand, and that is death. So they always have to depart from the human body they have invaded before it is afflicted by death. This is again and again a bitter disappointment for them, for what they so much want to succeed in is to remain in the human body beyond death. In their own kingdom this would be a high achievement for these beings; but so far they have failed in this.

If the Mystery of Golgotha had not taken place, if Christ had not passed through the Mystery of Golgotha, these beings would long since have gained the ability on earth to remain in the human body after a karmically pre-determined death. They would then have gained control over human evolution on earth and would have become the masters of this human evolution on the earth.

It is of immensely profound importance for us to realize the connection between Christ's passage through the Mystery of Golgotha and these beings who want to conquer death in human nature but are as yet still unable to bear it. They must always take care not to be in the human being's body at the hour predetermined by that individual for his death; they must desist from maintaining that body beyond the hour of death and from lengthening the life in that body from lasting beyond that hour of death.

These matters have long been known to certain secret brotherhoods who are very well informed about these things yet have withheld this information from humanity at large—by what right we shall once again not investigate just now. But as things are today it is quite wrong to desist from gradually arming people with such concepts, for they will need them when they have stepped through the gate of death. Everything we experience here, including what lies beneath the threshold of consciousness, is needed by us after death when we have to look back to this life and in this looking back must comprehend it, for being unable to do this is the worst thing that can happen to us. But our concepts for understanding this life as we look back over it are insufficient if we cannot throw light on a being who plays such a part in our life as does this ahrimanic being who takes possession of us before birth and is ever-present as a feature of our subconscious. Our concepts for understanding this life are insufficient if we cannot throw light on these things; for wisdom is transformed into light after we die.

These beings are very important for human life in every respect, and knowledge of them must and will gradually take hold in humanity. But this knowledge must take hold of people in the right way and cannot be allowed to be spread around by secret brotherhoods who want to use it as a way of increasing their power; nor, above all, may it be permitted to be kept secret as a means of increasing the power of certain brotherhoods who work egoistically.

Humanity is striving to gain all-round knowledge and such knowledge must be allowed to spread, for in future it will not be beneficial if secret brotherhoods can use such things as a means of spreading their own influence. Knowledge of these beings will increasingly have to take hold in humanity over the coming centuries. Over the coming centuries human beings will increasingly need to know that they bear a double within them, an ahrimanic, mephistophelian double. Human beings need to know this. Already they are developing a number of concepts which, however, remain rather meaningless because people do not yet know what to do about them. People are developing concepts which can only be properly comprehended once they are linked with the facts that underlie them.

Something is opening up here which will in future definitely have to be pursued if humanity is not to meet with endless hindrances, endless frightful happenings. This double of whom I have been speaking is neither more nor less than the originator of all physical diseases that arise spontaneously from within, and to know this being fully is what is meant by organic medicine. Diseases that come spontaneously from within, not those caused by external injuries, do not come from the soul but from this being who is the originator of all organic diseases that arise spontaneously from within. This being is the originator of all organic diseases, while his brother, whose nature is luciferic rather than ahrimanic, is the originator of all neuro-psychological and neurotic diseases, all diseases which are not really diseases at all but merely, as one says, nervous diseases, hysterical diseases and so on.

So medicine must become spiritual in two directions. The fact that this is required is shown, as I mentioned in Zurich,[6] by the way psychoanalysis, together with other ways of thinking, is coming to the fore, although it involves having to deal with spiritual entities while not knowing enough about them. So one is at a loss as to how to deal with phenomena that are entering more and more into human life. It will thus be necessary for certain things to happen. Even things that may be harmful in one respect must happen because people need to be exposed to this harm in order to overcome it and gain strength by doing so.

In order fully to understand all the things about which I have been speaking — that the double is the originator of all organic as opposed to merely functional diseases — one must know many other things as well. For example one must know that our earth is not the dead object described today in mineralogy or geology, but a living being. Mineralogy or geology know of the earth as much as we would know of a person if we were familiar solely with the skeleton. Imagine never being able to see people with your senses but only by means of X-rays; think of being familiar only with someone's skeleton. If this were the case, you would know of the person as much as geologists, and indeed science as such, know about the earth. Imagine coming in here and seeing nothing but the bones of all the members of our respected audience; you would then know as much about those present here as today's science knows about the earth.

The earth which is known only as a skeleton is, in reality, a living organism; and as a living organism it influences the beings who move about upon it, namely, human beings themselves. Just as a human being is differentiated in the way his organs are distributed around his body, so is the earth differentiated in what it develops within it, which in turn influences the human beings moving about upon it. I expect you are aware of this when you consider that to think will necessitate using your head and not your right forefinger or the big toe on your left foot. You know perfectly well that you do not think with the big toe on your right foot but with your head. Different things are distributed throughout a living organism; such an organism is differentiated.

And the earth is differentiated in the same way. Our earth is certainly not a being that sends up the same emanations to its inhabitants wherever they may be. All kinds of different emanations come up out of the earth in different regions. There are various forces, magnetic, electrical and so on, but also a great deal more in the living realm which rise up out of the earth and influence human beings in manifold ways at different places on its surface.

The influences on people vary depending on the geographical formations.

This is an exceedingly important fact. There are few direct connections between the emanations rising up out of the earth and the human being in his configuration of body, soul and spirit. But the double about whom I have been speaking is pre-eminently connected with the forces that stream up out of the earth. And because of this most intimate relationship between the double and what thus rises up, the human being in body, soul and spirit is indirectly also connected with the earth and what emanates from it in different regions. These doubles who, as ahrimanic-mephistophelian beings, take possession of human beings a short time before they are born are partial in their nature to quite distinct flavours. There are those who are particularly partial to the eastern hemisphere comprising Europe, Asia and Africa and therefore choose human beings who go there to be born and use their bodies. Others choose bodies born in the western hemisphere, in America. What we as human beings possess in a faint image as geography is experienced by these beings as a living principle in accordance with which they choose their domicile.

So you can see that one of the most important tasks of the future will be the cultivation of geographic medicine, medical geography, which through Paracelsus[7] broke away from the old, atavistic wisdom. Materialistic views have meant that since then it has received little cultivation. But it will gain ground once more when people get to know about the links between that being who makes human beings ill and the earth's geography—all those fusions and emanations that emerge from this earth in its various regions. It is indeed important for people to get to know about these things, for their very life depends on them. Through their double they find themselves situated in earthly existence in a specific way, and this double has its dwelling place within them.

These things have only really become so immeasurably important during the course of the fifth post-Atlantean epoch, and they will be especially important for humanity in the very near future. That is why spiritual science must now be made more widely known. This is particularly important because our age is calling on people to come to grips consciously with these things and relate to them in a conscious way. Human beings must be strong in this day and age in order to bring order into their relationship with these beings.

The present epoch began in the fifteenth century, in 1413. The fourth post-Atlantean epoch, the Graeco-Roman age, began before the Mystery of Golgotha in 747 BC and lasted until AD 1413. Since then we have been living in the fifth post-Atlantean age. Its characteristics, which have been in preparation since the fifteenth century, are only now coming fully to the fore. During the fourth post-Atlantean epoch it was the intellectual or mind soul which chiefly developed, whereas now it is the consciousness soul that is developing within human evolution as a whole.

When human beings entered this age it was their specific weakness with regard to the double which the leading spiritual beings had to take into account. If they had taken into their consciousness very much of all that is connected with the double they would have fared badly, very badly. Even during the centuries preceding the fourteenth century they had to be protected in advance so that they would take in only very little that might in any way recall the double. That is why knowledge about the double, which certainly existed in more ancient times, came to be lost. People had to be protected not only against becoming aware of anything regarding the double as far as any theory about it went, but also so that they would come into contact as little as possible with anything to do with it.

Something quite specific had to be arranged in order to achieve this. Try to understand this. During the centuries preceding the fourteenth century people had to be protected against the double. The double had to disappear from people's view and has only been permitted to reappear now in our age when human beings must bring order into their relationship with it. For the double to disappear from people's view a very significant arrangement had to be carried out which it was only possible to set in train in the following way. Gradually from the ninth, the tenth century onwards the situation was created in Europe that caused Europeans to lose a certain contact which they had previously had, a contact that had been important for people of an earlier time, during the seventh, the sixth post-Christian centuries. Beginning from the ninth century and reaching a culmination in the twelfth all traffic with America, such as was possible with the ships of the time, was discontinued.

This will no doubt sound rather strange to you, and you are likely to exclaim that history has never told you of such a thing! Well, in many ways history is a legend. For in centuries of European development long ago ships did indeed set off from Norway, from what was then Norway, to America. Of course it had a different name then and was not called America.

People knew about the region in America where especially those magnetic forces rise up which bring human beings into a relationship with the double. The most noticeable relations with the double emanate from that part of the earth which is covered by the American continent. And in those early centuries people sailed in Norwegian boats to America where they then studied diseases. Coming from Europe, people went to America to study the diseases caused by the earth's magnetism. That is where we can find the mysterious origin of ancient European medicine. That is where it was possible to observe the course of diseases, which would not have been possible in Europe where people were more susceptible to the influences of the double.

Gradually it became necessary — and most of this was achieved by means of the edicts issued by the Roman Catholic Church — to make people forget the connection to America. And it was then not until the beginning of the fifth post-Atlantean epoch that America was rediscovered in a physical, sense-perceptible way. In fact this was only a rediscovery, but it is nonetheless significant in the way it shows that the powers who had been at work had indeed succeeded in ensuring that nothing much at all concerning Europe's earlier connections with America was to be found in old records; and where there is some mention it is not recognized for what it is, so that people do not realize that it refers to links between Europe and America in times long gone. The visits made in those ancient days were actually more than visits although the Europeans did not become an American people in the way this became possible after the physical discovery, the physical rediscovery of America. In those early times the Europeans visited in order to study what a very special role was played by the double in the race of the American Indians, who were different from them.

For a while, before the fifth post-Atlantean time began to develop, Europe had to be protected against influences from the western world. That is the significant historical arrangement that had to be set in train by wisdom-filled world powers. For a time Europe had to be protected against all those influences, and this protection would have been impossible if the European world had not been totally closed in and shut off from America during the centuries that preceded the fifteenth century.

During those preparatory centuries it was necessary for a time to be very subtle in the way certain things were presented to the humanity of Europe. What I mean to say is that the understanding that was to gain ground pre-eminently during this fifth post-Atlantean age had to be very tenderly nurtured when it first appeared. What was to be revealed in that understanding had to be brought in with the utmost subtlety. Sometimes that subtlety was of course like the subtlety in education when in certain circumstances quite considerable punishment has to be meted out. But what I am talking about now refers to the grand impulses of history.

Thus it came about that Irish monks — under the influence of the pure Christian esoteric doctrine that was forming in Ireland — worked in a way that persuaded Rome of the necessity to close Europe off from the western hemisphere. It was from Ireland that the movement emanated which, during the centuries prior to the fifth post-Atlantean epoch, sought to spread Christianity in Europe in a way that would leave it undisturbed by everything rising up out of the subterranean regions of the earth in the western hemisphere.

This is perhaps a good point at which to say a few words about these things. Columban[8] and St Gall[9] were pre-eminent individuals in that great and important missionary effort which sought to christianize Europe by surrounding it with spiritual walls so that no influences of the kind I have described would come in. Individuals like Columban and his pupil Gall—to whom this place here owes its foundation and its name—realized that the delicate plant of christianization could only spread in Europe if Europe were surrounded by a kind of fence, spiritually speaking. There are indeed profound and significant secrets hidden behind the processes of world history, and the history taught in our schools is in many ways a legend.

Among the most important facts to be taken into account in an effort to understand more recent times in Europe is this. From the centuries during which Christianity was spread from Ireland throughout Europe, right up to the twelfth century, efforts were made, especially by means of the papal edicts, to place a taboo on maritime traffic between Europe and America and put a stop to it, so that the links between America and Europe came to be completely forgotten. This forgetting was necessary so that the first period of the development of the fifth post-Atlantean era in Europe should be worked through in the right way. Only when the age of materialism began was America rediscovered. Then America was discovered under the influence of the greed for gold, under the influence of a purely materialistic culture with which people have to reckon in the fifth post-Atlantean era and with which they must establish an appropriate relationship.

These are the things that are genuine history. And they are what throw light on what is real. The earth has to be described as a living being. It has geographical differentiations in the way the most varied forces stream up out of all kinds of different terrestrial regions. That is why human beings must not be separated off according to terrestrial region but must take on from one another whatever each region can uniquely produce in the way of what is good and great. And that is why the world view of spiritual science is mindful of the need to create something that can be truly accepted by all nations in all regions. Human beings must progress through a mutual exchange of their spiritual riches. It is this that is crucial.

Individual terrestrial regions, on the other hand, easily engender the endeavour to increase power and power and more power. The great danger of newer human evolution going forward in a one-sided way can only be assessed on the basis of concrete, really concrete conditions if one knows about the earth being an organism and if one knows what is really emanating from different points on the globe.

In the eastern part of Europe there is relatively little tendency with regard to power because for Russians, for example, although they are intimately bound up with the soil, the special forces that have to be taken up from the ground are forces which do not stem from the earth. The mystery of Russian geography tells us that what Russians take up out of the earth is first and foremost the light which has been bestowed on the earth and is then given back. So Russians absorb from the earth something that has streamed into it from outer regions. Russians love their soil, but they love it because for them it mirrors the heavens. So however terrestrial or territorial their cast of mind might be, this territorial attitude—although at present remaining at a childlike level—is extraordinarily cosmopolitan because as the earth moves through space it comes into touch with all the many parts of its surroundings.

To take into the soul not what streams in the earth from below upwards but what first came from above downwards and then streams upwards again from below is different from taking in something which, in that it streams up directly out of the earth, is given a certain kinship with human nature. What Russians love about their soil, what fills them to the brim, gives them a good many weaknesses, but it also gives them some ability to overcome that nature of the double about which I was speaking just now. So it will be the Russians who will be called upon to provide the most important impulses in the age when the time will finally have come to do battle with that double, namely, in the sixth post-Atlantean era.

There is one specific part of the earth's underlying ground which has the greatest kinship with those forces. When people go there they enter into that sphere of influence, but when they go away again they are no longer influenced in that way. These are geographical forces; this is not a matter of ethnicity or nationality but purely of geography. The region where that which streams upwards from below has the greatest influence on the double and where, because of this kinship with the double it reflects back to the earth as well, this is the region where most of the mountain ranges do not cross from west to east but run mainly from north to south, where the magnetic North Pole is nearby—for this, too, is connected with those forces. This is the region where, through the prevailing external conditions, above all a kinship is developed with the mephistophelian-ahrimanic nature. This kinship has many effects on the further development of the earth. So people must not go along blindly with the earth's development, for they must see and understand these conditions.

Europe will only be able to enter into a right relationship with America when such conditions are seen and understood, when people know which geographical conditions are determining what comes from there. But if Europe persists in being blind to these things, then this unfortunate

Europe's fate will be like the fate of Greece with regard to Rome. This must not be allowed to happen; the world must not be allowed to become geographically Americanized. But this presupposes that we understand what is meant. Things must be taken far more seriously than is frequently the case today. What happens is based on deep foundations; so knowledge is needed, and not merely sympathies and antipathies, in order to gain a stance with regard to the circumstances in which present-day humanity so tragically finds itself now.

We can speak in more detail about these things here, whereas this isn't possible in public lectures. Yesterday I mentioned the importance of bringing spiritual science right into social and political concepts,[10] for it is America's endeavour to mechanize everything, to push everything into the realm of pure naturalism, thus gradually extinguishing Europe's culture altogether.

Of course the concepts I am referring to are geographical, not national. You need only think of someone like Emerson in order to realize that what I am referring to is not a matter of national characteristics.[11] Emerson was a human being thoroughly steeped in the culture of Europe. As you see, there are two opposing poles that are evolving. Under the very influences I have been speaking about today some develop like Emerson and confront the double with their full humanity while others develop like Woodrow Wilson[12] and become merely a garment for the double, so that the double works particularly strongly through them. These latter are like embodiments of America's geographical nature.

All this has nothing to do with any kind of sympathy or antipathy nor with taking sides in any way. It is to do with knowing about the deeper reasons for what people live through during their lives. Humanity will not find much help if it fails to reach clarity about what is actually at work. Today it is very necessary to reconnect with much that had to be severed at the turning-point when the way to America was barred. Human beings like St Gall can stand as symbols of what you can experience and feel in this connection. They had to create a foundation for their work by means of the barrier they set up. These are things that one must understand.

It is spiritual science that can create genuine historical understanding. But as you see, it will of course be met by prejudice after prejudice, for what can one expect but that knowledge will be made to support the views of one party or another! This was one of the reasons for the cowardice that made certain secret brotherhoods hold back with these things. They held back for the simple reason that people often find knowledge uncomfortable, for they do not want to become generally human. This applies particularly to those who have an inclination to link up with the geographical forces streaming up out of the earth.

Matters of public life will, surely, gradually become questions of knowledge and be lifted out of the atmosphere—out of the sphere of mere sympathies and antipathies—into which they are being forced today by the great majority of humanity. It will, though, not be majorities that decide what is effective. But what is effective will only be able to be effective if people stop shying away from taking important matters into their consciousness.

What I have spoken about today because—if I might put it like this—the *genius loci* of this place expected it of me, has been based on a specific example, namely, the fact that to get to know history it is now no longer sufficient for people to consult the usual historical textbooks, since what these tell us in the name of history is nothing but a legend. What do they tell us about the important seafaring routes which lie at the hidden root of medicine and which people followed from Europe to America even in the early centuries of Christianity? Yet what exists does not cease to exist if people later on make their consciousness blind to it like ostriches burying their heads in the sand and then believing that what they cannot see does not exist. Many other things, too, are now hidden from view by that legend which people call history, things that are now quite close to what present-day people do. Many things about the course of human history will be brought out into the light by spiritual science. For people want to be enlightened about their own destiny and about how their soul is linked with their spiritual development.

Much, then, that has been lost to history can only be rediscovered by spiritual science. Or else humanity will have to decide to remain in the dark even about some matters that are very relevant. Spiritual science alone can provide a standpoint from which to judge the present time even though we are all so exceedingly well informed about it. But how, exactly, are we so well informed? With all due respect—as one says nowadays when one intends to say something impolite—with all due respect, it is the press that informs us by disguising the very aspects that are essential, true and real, in other words: the aspects that matter.

Yet people need to reach this degree of reality in what they know. This is not meant as a criticism of the press either personally or impersonally, but it is meant as a statement about something that is at work in the present time, something that cannot help being as it is. Things cannot be other than they are, but people must be aware of this. It is a great mistake to believe that one must criticize things, for what one must do is characterize them; that is what matters.

Today I have tried to give you a picture of certain impulses at work in the individual human being and in humanity as a whole. Apart from the specific details I have mentioned I also wanted the type of impulses I have touched on to give you above all a sense of how human beings must be aware that with their whole being they are embedded in a real spiritual world filled with real spiritual beings and real spiritual forces. Not only do we wake up into that world into which we step after death and in which we live between death and a new birth, but we also learn to understand the physical world by being in it while knowing about the spiritual world at the same time. We can only understand the physical world if we also understand the spiritual world.

Medicine can only endure if it is a spiritual science. Diseases come from a spiritual being that is only using the human body in order to find its due which it cannot find at the place intended for it by the wisdom-filled leadership of the world against which it has rebelled, as I have shown. It is a being, actually an ahrimanic-mephistophelian being, living in the human being's physical nature, a being who takes the human body as its domicile before birth and who only leaves this human body because it must not be allowed to endure death under the circumstances holding sway in the present time, and because also it cannot conquer death. Diseases arise because this being works in the human being. The purpose of using medical remedies is to give this being something belonging to the external world, something which it otherwise seeks to find through the human being. By giving the human body a medical remedy when that ahrimanic-mephistophelian being is at work there I am giving it something else; I am as though caressing that being, reconciling it so that it leaves the human being in peace and gains satisfaction instead from the medical remedy I am throwing down its throat.

But we are only at the very beginning of all these things. Medicine will become a spiritual science. And just as medicine was known to be a spiritual science in olden times, so will it come to be recognized as such again.

Another feeling that I will have awoken in you is that it is necessary not only to acquire a few concepts from spiritual science but also to feel one's way into it. By doing this one also feels one's way into the human being. The time has come when the scales will fall from our eyes in many respects, for example also in respect of external history. A few days ago in Zurich I proved, or rather showed, that history is not viewed by us from outside but that we dream it in reality, and that we only understand it if we take it as belonging to the dream of humanity and not as something or other that runs its course in the outer world.[13]

It is to be hoped that these things will also be carried further by the power that has so far taken hold only of quite a small, an all too small section of humanity in what we call the anthroposophical movement. This anthroposophical movement will nevertheless be connected with all that will have to lead humanity to its most important affairs in the future. We have often remembered a comparison I have frequently drawn.[14] The clever people out there think to themselves: Well, all those anthroposophists and theosophists, they are one of those sects with all kinds of fantastic stuff and foolish ideas in their heads; those of us who belong to the enlightened section of humanity should take care to have nothing to do with them! With modifications owing to the fact that time has moved on, that 'enlightened section of humanity' is thinking along the same lines about these subterranean, sectarian assemblages of anthroposophists and theosophists as did the Romans, the distinguished Romans, when Christianity first began to spread. The Christians of those times actually had to descend into physical catacombs while up above them all the things went on which those distinguished Romans considered right and proper while those fantastical Christians were down below. But once a few centuries had passed things had changed. The Roman world had been swept away and what had been down below in the catacombs had risen to the surface. What had once dominated culture had been torn up by its roots.

Such comparisons must strengthen our resolve; such comparisons must take up residence in our souls so that we can draw strength from them while we still have to work in such small circles. The movement characterized by this anthroposophical stream must develop the strength that can really come up from below, even though up here little understanding for its spiritual foundations awaits it.

Nevertheless we must not cease thinking back to happenings like the existence of the early Christians in the catacombs which, even though it was far more subterranean than is the anthroposophical movement today, still found its way up to the surface. Some of those who wrestle with spiritual concepts in this anthroposophical movement have already found the possibility of working with that light in the sphere where spiritual concepts, which are wisdom here, unfold as light. We are able to repeat again and again that among the members who work in the anthroposophical movement we are as close to those who are here in the physical world as we are to those who are already over there in the supersensible world, having stepped through the gate of death. Over there today they bear out the truth of what is gained here by way of spiritual wisdom. There are already a good many member souls living in the supersensible world about whom we should be thinking.

At this moment I am thinking once again about Sophie Stinde, who worked so faithfullly at the Goetheanum, because the anniversary of her physical death is approaching again, her supersensible birthday into spiritual life.[15] Dear friends, if we truly wish to take our place in the positive anthroposophical movement, what we have to do is deepen the feeling that tells us: Through what is genuinely connected with us we take in the concrete concept of the spiritual world ...[16]

So, dear friends, times are difficult indeed. We know how hard it will be to get through the coming weeks. Whatever may happen as regards our meeting again on the physical plane, however long or short the time may be until we can come together again here, let me say to you that in order to preserve and strengthen our endeavours in spiritual science we shall, despite everything, feel ourselves to be together and think ourselves to be together even though we are separate from one another in space. Let us remain always together as those who strive in spiritual science ...[17]

3. *Behind the Scenes of External Events, I*

Many years ago[1] when I was working in Berlin and happened to be at a play, news of the assassination, by an
anarchist, of the Empress of Austria in Geneva was as
though wafted into the theatre during the performance.[2] As
this news came wafting in during an interval I found myself
standing near a man who was then a theatre critic in Berlin
but has since written well-known philosophical books.[3] He
was expressing his astonishment in rather a memorable
fashion. He said: 'You can be understanding about many
things in the world even if you find them unjustified and
don't agree with them, but'—so said the man—'it's
incomprehensible and serves no purpose for an activist
movement to kill a sick woman whose continued life could
not have changed things in any important way and whose
death had no obvious connection with any political ideas.'

I think that man was expressing an opinion that must
surely be that of any sensible person in today's educated
world. Therefore we might draw the conclusion that things
happen amongst human beings, things happen during the
course of historical events that appear senseless when
measured by the normal standards of life, things that even
appear senseless if we try to explain them as some kind of
mistake.

However, this is the very kind of event—and we could
add many, many more to the list—which shows us that
something seemingly incomprehensible outwardly must

indeed appear incomprehensible outwardly because there are spiritual forces and spiritual deeds being played out both for good and evil behind the scenes, if I may use this expression, of events in world history—spiritual happenings and spiritual actions which can only be comprehended if spiritual science can be used to throw light on the realms that lie behind the scenery of everyday life as it runs its course in the sense-perceptible world. These things that happen can only be comprehended on the basis of ideas from the spiritual world and they must of necessity appear incomprehensible, whether in a good or an evil sense, if they are viewed only in connection with the sense-perceptible world. So if one has an experience like this one in a theatre, which might be called a coincidence but could perhaps also be a symbolic guise for something karmic, then one is inclined to ponder on how different things look behind the scenes in comparison with what is being presented on the stage.

These remarks are intended as a starting-point for what I want to say today, which I shall also enlarge on further the next time we gather here. I shall talk now about what it is important for people to know in connection with all kinds of things that take place behind the scenery of events here on the physical plane. If one wanted to fit in with today's lazy way of describing only in general terms what lives in the spiritual world and is connected with human affairs here on earth, one would be unable to make them comprehensible, for we can only understand these things if we go right into concrete, actual facts of the spiritual world.

As you know—and as has been described and written about many times[4]—we structure human evolution according to different periods: great periods such as the old Saturn, Sun and Moon times and so on, and smaller periods such as the Lemurian and Atlantean ages and our post-Atlantean period. Even these smaller periods are tremendously long, and within them we speak of cultural epochs, which for our post-Atlantean period are the ancient Indian, ancient Persian, the Egypto-Chaldean, the Graeco-Latin epochs and our present fifth post-Atlantean age.

We speak of these periods because in progressing through earthly evolution humanity as a whole changes its — in this case soul — characteristics from one period to the next; humanity undergoes a real development in each such period (by which I now mean the smallest of the periods mentioned). Every such period imposes obligations on humanity as to what must be experienced, what must cause joy or sorrow, what must be learned, where the source of its will impulses lies, and so on. The task to be tackled by the Egypto-Chaldean cultural epoch differed from that facing the Graeco-Latin one, and our own age also has quite specific tasks.

We can properly view the differences in the tasks facing these successive epochs with regard to the characteristics to be developed (specifically those to be discussed today), we can view these properly if we try to include in our considerations the experiences that belong to human life as a *whole*, and not only those that are important for external evolution to which today's materialistic view wants to restrict itself. What is experienced externally by human beings on the physical plane is only one part of overall human life which takes its course not only between birth and death but also between death and a new birth. Life on the physical earth does not on its own give us the full picture of the successive epochs. In reality the forces from the realm in which human beings spend their time between death and a new birth always come down and interact with the forces unfolded by them while they are here on the physical plane. What is involved is always an interplay between the forces unfolded by human beings after death and those which they unfold here on the physical plane.

Throughout the whole period of the fourth post-Atlantean epoch it was in order for human beings to be kept unaware about certain things. But many of the things about which the people of the fourth post-Atlantean epoch, the Graeco-Latin epoch, could be kept unaware are the very ones of which the human beings of the fifth post-Atlantean epoch must become more and more conscious. In fact, this fifth post-Atlantean age will anyway be one in which much that was formerly outside consciousness will have to enter into the consciousness of human souls.

Such developments take place in accordance with certain spiritual laws; they are governed by a certain spiritual necessity. Humanity is simply predisposed in such a way that certain capacities of understanding and also certain forces of will develop at a specific time. During the fifth post-Atlantean age humanity will become ready for certain things just as it became ready for other things in earlier periods. Humanity becomes ready for these things. One such matter for which the humanity of this fifth post-Atlantean age is becoming ready is something that people today find especially paradoxical because a large part of today's public opinion is striving in the very opposite direction and is wanting to guide people in this opposite direction. But it cannot be avoided. The spiritual forces that are inoculated into humanity, if I may use this phrase, during the course of the fifth post-Atlantean period will be stronger than certain people will wish and stronger than what public opinion expects.

One matter that will assert itself powerfully will be the

possibility for humanity to be guided more in accordance
with occult principles than has ever been the case before. It
is characteristic of this development that during this fifth
post-Atlantean age certain conditions of power, certain
strong capacities to be influential must become con-
centrated in small groups of people who will have much
power over other, larger masses.

Part of today's public opinion is working strongly to
counteract this, but it will develop anyway—for a specific
reason. It will develop because during the fifth post-
Atlantean age a large part of humanity will, out of what is
maturing in its soul, out of what is necessary for the evolution of humanity, develop certain spiritual capacities,
namely, a certain natural ability to look into the spiritual
world. This part of humanity will certainly represent the
best basis for what is to come in the sixth post-Atlantean
age, the age that will follow our present one, but in the fifth
post-Atlantean age during which it is making these preparations, this part of humanity will have little inclination to
turn its attention strongly to matters of the physical plane. It
will be concerning itself a great deal with bringing the life of
heart and soul on to a higher level and putting certain
spiritual matters in order. And because of this others, who
are rather less suited to such spiritual life, will be enabled to
seize certain conditions of power for themselves.

There is a degree of inevitability about this. And it is
something that was much discussed during the final third
of the nineteenth century in those circles who know about
such things. There was constant discussion of the urgent
necessity to ensure that this possibility should be guided
not into evil but into good paths. During the final third of
the nineteenth century, and especially as the turn to the
twentieth century was approaching, occultists of every

persuasion were heard to say: Preparations must be made so that those who attain the power to act may be the ones who are worthy of it. Obviously, except in the case of very few circles, those closest to the speaker for whatever worldly reason were the ones seen as worthy. Amongst occultists this subject was as topical then as it is in a certain sense today.

There are other things, too, that will come out and become known to people and enter into their will during the fifth post-Atlantean age simply because human beings have reached the stage in their development where they are ready for them. These things are more far-reaching, in fact they are so far-reaching that they must be of serious concern to all those who are conversant with such matters.

During the fifth post-Atlantean epoch the human being's physical apparatus for thinking will become mature enough to comprehend fully certain elements connected with diseases, certain processes of healing and connections between natural processes and diseases. Those who know about these matters are concerned because they must adopt the goal of ensuring that the individuals who will be chosen to bring teachings and impulses about such things out into the open will do so in a proper and dignified manner. For there will be two possibilities. Either it will be possible to put out information about these things in a way that leads to calamity for the world or it will be possible for them to be taught in a way that leads to welfare in the world. These things are connected with the inmost essence of certain conditions in human procreation and certain conditions connected with diseases, and also with certain conditions relating to the advent of death. By being made known to humanity, these things become weighty thoughts and impulses and are very significant indeed. Meanwhile, the purpose of this fifth post-Atlantean age is to bring the degree of freedom to human beings which they will need in order to receive enlightenment about certain matters that have hitherto lived more in the subconscious realm of their soul and also to enable them to master these things.

Those who know about such things have been at great pains to consider what is feasible or can be done in the one or the other direction, for everything that can be done in these matters conveys a degree of power and a possibility of participating in human affairs in far-reaching ways. With regard to the development of the fifth post-Atlantean age these matters have, as I mentioned earlier, been very much to the fore within the esoteric streams of the nineteenth century right up to our own time.

There is also another fact that those who know about it regard as very important, so that because of its importance they must bring it into connection with various others. I have mentioned this in lectures from time to time.[5] When you have stepped across the threshold to the spiritual world and are making spiritual observations there, you find that single facts, always individual facts, appear before your soul. It then transpires that facts which at first sight appear to the spiritual eye to have nothing to do with one another are actually connected when you grasp their meaning. Such facts illumine and clarify each other and then enable you to press on further into the essence of the spiritual world in the profoundest sense.

A further fact which I also want to put before you will at first sight appear completely unconnected with what I have just said, but you will find that this further fact does actually have very much, a very great deal to do with those things I have just mentioned. This further fact is this. On turning today to the souls of human beings who have died and on becoming acquainted with what I might call their 'life situations' we find that there are some among them who are extremely worried after death about becoming acquainted with those souls who met their earthly end in situations like that which befell the Empress of Austria in Geneva.[6] In other words, we discover that those who are sent through the gate of death by activists — let us call them this for the moment — represent a great worry for some others, who have passed through the gate of death in the normal way and then gone on to have their experiences in the spiritual world. We find that human souls who have passed through the gate of death in the normal way dread, after death, having anything to do with those other souls; they avoid having contact with them.

Please do not in this case dwell on what must seem to your feelings to be paradoxical about this reaction. There are of course so many ways in which souls can meet and have dealings with one another that it would be misplaced to bring our sympathy into play immediately even though this would be a justifiable and understandable way to react in such a situation. We have to look objectively at the facts in a case like this. And the fact here is that souls who have had a normal passage through the gate of death shy away from souls who have been guided through the gate of death by the deeds of activists.

These two things, this last-mentioned fact and what I explained before, are linked, and the link is quite specific. On looking more closely we find that the souls who have been violently propelled through the gate of death know something in the spiritual world after death which the other souls do not want to learn about from them at the wrong time; they do not want to learn about it sooner than would be beneficial. The situation is that the souls who have passed violently through the gate of death retain something on account of having lost their life in that way here in the physical world; they have retained certain possibilities of being able to make use of forces which they have had here, for instance the force of the intellect. So from over there, from the spiritual side, these souls can use the forces that are bound to the physical body and do quite different things with them than can be done with them here in the physical body. This enables them to know certain things sooner than is actually beneficial in the overall process of human evolution.

Thus it is remarkable that what appears to be mean-ingless, namely, a number of those actions by activists, is now revealed to have a meaning, albeit a very dubious one. To those who understand what is going on these acts appear in rather a strange light. Here in the physical world we say a lot of nonsensical things that are supposed to be meaningful but do not mean anything on closer inspection. Here in the physical world we say: These people, these activists who murder people, are only doing it in order to draw attention to the misery in the world; it is a means of incitement and so on. But if you analyse the matter and try to bring it into the context of social laws you notice im-mediately that none of this has any meaning. It becomes meaningful, however, if you know that souls sent up into the spiritual world by such means understand things up there which they ought not to understand yet and which souls who have died in the normal way even shy away from.

Of course what then suggests itself is that, on the basis of information such as is available regarding the murder of the Empress Elisabeth of Austria, one should investigate eso-terically the various assassinations that have been taking place, so as to discover what is going on in connection with those souls who arrive in the spiritual world as the keepers, as it were, of certain secrets that can have consequences about which we shall speak in a moment. Those who examine the sequence of these assassinations purely externally are likely to conclude that the selection has come about by chance. But if you analyse the matter and look at the individuals who have been dispatched to their death in this way you realize that they must have been selected on purpose, though not on the basis of criteria applying to the physical world but rather on the basis of criteria applying to the spiritual world.

However, on investigating a large number of known assassinations with this in mind one comes up with something very peculiar. On looking at Carnot,[7] at the Empress Elisabeth and a good many others, something very peculiar becomes evident. What becomes evident is that although, as I have described, there was a possibility of achieving something through these assassinations, it has not been achieved; nothing of it has been achieved. It would have been achieved if souls had been found who would, so to speak, have been willing to receive what was on offer. Both parties would then have been involved in a transcendental, a supersensible guilt. The souls who had passed through death in the normal way would have learned about things which would have driven them in directions through which they would have become guilty; and those who had gone into death violently, by means of assassinations, would have made themselves guilty through having disclosed something which it is not yet possible to disclose.

Higher spiritual beings, higher hierarchies prevented this because from a certain point of view the consequences would have been such that they needed to be averted for the good of a certain portion of humanity. The damage that would have been done by these things was prevented, so to speak, by the intervention of higher spiritual beings. So what we find here is an attempt made with unsuitable means or means that were deprived of their suitability, an attempt to do something in the spiritual world behind the scenes of our usual, physical world.

On delving even further into these matters we find the source of these impulses. In the greater part of the assassinations that have become known to you, and have been discussed in Europe, the impulses, by which I mean the spiritual impulses, were not the original ones; they were derived from something else. They were, to put it simply, measures of defence. The purpose was to avert something else. These deeds were intended as a way of preventing other deeds along the same lines from being carried out, or rather of preventing the consequences of such deeds from taking effect.

This is a very mysterious matter. And this whole matter only becomes comprehensible if we consider what it was that had to be prevented, what it was against which these preventive measures had to be taken. We are looking here through spiritual science into matters that are profoundly connected with the impulses of present and future human life about which it is extraordinarily difficult to speak because everywhere they go against certain naïve, and also justified, interests that people have. This whole matter only becomes comprehensible when we bear in mind that everything I have so far told you, that all these ventures of assassination I have so far mentioned were actually guided amateurishly in a dilettante fashion, without thorough knowledge of the occult circumstances, because they were born out of a kind of fear as preventive measures and were also not guided uniformly. This whole matter only becomes comprehensible if we examine what it was that had to be deflected. As such, this has already been striven for and set in motion by means involving greater insight.

Right up into the nineteenth century there existed in the East a remarkable order, the Thugs. This order, which flourished in a part of Asia, had not come into being simply out of the longing in the hearts of its members to achieve certain aims. The members of this order were obliged to murder certain individuals indicated to them by superiors who very, very strongly maintained their anonymity. The order was a kind of murderers' order which had the task of murdering certain individuals. Its activity simply manifested in the way one heard from time to time that one person or another had been murdered. The murder was committed when a member of the order of Thugs was instructed by anonymous superiors to murder such and such an individual.

Those in authority who set such things in train knew very well what goal they were pursuing. First they arranged the affairs of the physical plane in such a way that this order of murderers could come into being, and then they arranged the affairs of the order of murderers itself in such a way that its purposes could be carried out. The goal of all this was to make those human beings pass through the gate of death violently who would thus be equipped with the capacity that would enable them after death to know certain secrets. Those who arranged all this then also on the other hand set up here on the physical plane corresponding mirror events, as they are called in occult life. Their purpose is to set up corresponding mirror events here on the physical plane. Such events have indeed to some small extent already been set up here on the physical plane.

This is done as follows. Certain suitable individuals are schooled to be mediums. They are then put into a trance and the streams coming from the spiritual world are guided to the medium by certain methods in such a way that the medium makes known certain secrets that cannot be made known in any other way. The only way they can be made known is when a person who has been violently killed uses over in the other world certain forces which have remained usable as the result of the violent death; as a soul that person comes to understand the secrets and allows them to seep into the medium. Those here on earth who have an interest in finding out about such things can then find out more about what such souls allow to seep into the medium.

The things that are researched in this way are, in a sense, what I might call spiritual premature births. Souls who have passed through the gate of death in the normal way know, if they then meet with the opportunity to come into contact with such things, that their time has now come to prepare themselves, and they show that they are preparing themselves so that at a later time, when humanity will have reached the right stage of maturity, they will be ready to bring down certain matters from the spiritual world to the earth and inoculate them into the earth down here. Indeed, it is actually an important task for a number of people who are now passing through the gate of death to use—when they have become mature enough for certain secrets—the normal forces in connection with those secrets rather than learn about them through a foreshortened experience by using forces brought into play by a violent death. These human souls do indeed have the task of finding out about these forces and inspiring people who are here on the earth with them, people who are not mediums but who should find out about them in a normal and proper way through

Inspiration. In normal life one has to wait for this. When things that ought to come later make their appearance as spiritual premature births by the means I have described — through criminal occult activity — when this happens those whose intentions towards humanity are not good, in other words those who are black or grey magicians, can gain possession of such secrets.

Such things have indeed been going on behind the scenes of external events during the current decades. The purpose was, firstly, to present certain groups of people with the secret of how to dominate great masses, as I indicated first of all. This secret involves knowing how those masses who have little interest in external affairs, but who have budding spiritual capacities that can serve in preparing for the sixth post-Atlantean epoch, can be thoroughly dominated and how such domination can be put into the hands of some few individuals.

That was the first purpose. The other is something that will play a great part in the future, namely, to get those secrets into one's clutches for the purpose of turning in a certain direction the circumstances that have to do with the processes of disease, and also of procreation. I have already mentioned these things to a number of friends.[8] Certain circles in this materialistic age are striving to paralyse and make impossible all of humanity's spiritual development, through causing people by their very temperament and character to reject everything spiritual and regard it as nonsense.

A stream of this kind — and it is already noticeable in some isolated individuals — will become deeper and deeper. A longing will arise for there to be a general opinion: Whatever is spiritual, whatever is of the spirit, is nonsense, is madness! Endeavours to achieve this will be made by bringing out remedies to be administered by inoculation just as inoculations have been developed as a protection against diseases, only these inoculations will influence the human body in a way that will make it refuse to give a home to the spiritual inclinations of the soul. People will be inoculated against the inclination to entertain spiritual ideas. Endeavours in this direction will be made; inoculations will be tested that already in childhood will make people lose any urge for a spiritual life.

This is, however, only one of the things connected with a more intimate knowledge that must come about in this fifth post-Atlantean age regarding the connection of these natural processes and remedies with the human organism. They will make their appearance among humanity at the appropriate time. The decisive question will be what succeeds first, whether the endeavours to let those spiritual premature births get into the hands of individuals for the furtherance of their own purposes, or whether knowledge about these things will come down in the right way for the welfare of humanity when the time is ripe.

The organization intending to bring about those spiritual premature births through working with the help of the Thug order of murderers was not amateurish. It worked very systematically, but in a way that is frightful for anyone whose intentions towards humanity are beneficial. It worked professionally, not amateurishly, and knew all about the appropriate means.

Because there were these endeavours to bring down too early from the spiritual world by certain means something that must come during the course of human maturity in the fifth post-Atlantean age, and get it into the egoistic possession of a part of humanity, there then arose the anxious uneasiness in others which came to the fore like a counter-image in the form of activism; but it was amateurish because it was born of fear. Its intention was to help, but its endeavours made use of unsuitable means.

What is going on behind the scenes of external events is very significant. These things would not be under discussion here today if there were not the binding need to draw them to the attention of those who are able to hear what is being said through having had some preparation in the matters of spiritual science. It is necessary for such things to enter into the consciousness of the humanity of the fifth post-Atlantean age. Only if they do enter into the consciousness of the humanity of the fifth post-Atlantean age will those things be achieved which must be the goal of earthly evolution.

The time must come when individuals take up the irksome task of thinking not only in the way thinking is taught by so-called educated people in the universities. A time must come when a number of individuals declare their willingness to take upon themselves this irksome view of the world which derives its direction, its concepts and its ideas out of the spiritual world. Humanity must not be allowed to remain in the dormant state it wants to retain with those abstract, generalized concepts not only striven for but also called noble by the materialistic age.

Anyway, when you consider what I have been pointing out you realize that there are a good many ways of using the streams coming over from the spiritual world in order to do harm here on the physical earth in the fifth post-Atlantean age; there are a number of possibilities for this, one of which I have pointed out today. And the fact that one must stress the need for some souls to absorb such knowledge consciously ties in with the whole fundamental character of our age.

The second half of the nineteenth century was a very important time. In one circle of our friends or another I have often pointed out that the year 1841 was a crisis year, a year of decision.[9] This is not obvious if you look only at the events which took place here in the physical world, for it is necessary to see these in conjunction with what is going on in the spiritual world. The year 1841 was indeed a critical year for the introduction of the materialistic age because that is when a certain battle began in the spiritual world, a battle of certain spirits of darkness, one might call it, who belong to the hierarchy of the Angeloi. They fought this battle in the spiritual world until the autumn of 1879. They had various specific aims of which we shall mention only one today. Between 1841 and 1879 the decision was to be taken as to whether a certain sum of spiritual wisdom could be brought to maturity in the spiritual world so that from the final third of the nineteenth century onwards it could gradually seep down to the earth and enter human souls and there stimulate spiritual knowledge, knowledge of the kind that today we call the knowledge of spiritual science. Such knowledge has only become possible since the final third of the nineteenth century.

The purpose of those Angeloi spirits between 1841 and 1879 was to prevent the maturing over there in the spiritual world of what was supposed to seep down. But those spirits lost the war they waged for decades against the spirits of light. In 1879 something then took place, on a smaller scale, which has taken place repeatedly during the course of evolution and has always been expressed by a particular symbol: Michael or St George triumphing over the dragon. In 1879, too, the dragon was overcome in a particular matter. The dragon was those Angeloi beings who strove for but failed to achieve what I have explained. So in 1879 they were thrown out of the spiritual world and into the realm of human beings. This was the fall of the Angeloi beings from the realm of the spiritual world into the realm of human beings; so now they move about here amongst human beings. They are here, sending their forces into the thoughts, feelings and will impulses of human beings by making mischief of one kind or another. By losing the battle they have failed to prevent the arrival of the time when the spiritual wisdom is filtering down. This spiritual wisdom is now here and will continue to develop ever more and more; and then human beings will have the ability to see and comprehend the spiritual world.

Those Angeloi beings have now fallen down to the earth. Here they want to do harm with what is filtering down; they want to guide the knowledge into the wrong channels, to rob it of its good powers and send it into bad channels. In short, having failed to achieve what they wanted with the help of spirits they now want to achieve it here with the help of human beings because of the fall they experienced in 1879. They want to destroy the good plan for the world which consists in spreading amongst human beings, when the right moment of maturity has been reached, the knowledge about how to control the masses, and the knowledge about birth, disease and death, and other things. They want to spread such knowledge too early, by means of those spiritual premature births. They are also busy in other ways, apart from what I have mentioned here.

Awareness alone will help us against the influence of these ahrimanic beings. I have pointed this out many times, especially in the Mystery Plays.[10] You will remember the final scene of the last one, where we see that the only thing which helps us to counteract Ahriman is to see through him, to know that he is there. The fifth post-Atlantean age must develop to the point at which many individuals can speak to the ahrimanic powers and beings as Faust does: 'For in thy Naught I trust to find the All.'[11] The attitude of mind must develop in which one can look into what the materialistic view sees as 'naught' and there see the spiritual world. If this happened, Ahriman-Mephistopheles would be forced to speak to such individuals as he speaks to Faust when he sends him to the Mothers: 'I will not grudge my praise before thou goest, and well I see that thou the Devil knowest.'[12] The other day over in Dornach I said in jest[13] that Mephistopheles would never have made such a remark to Woodrow Wilson![14] To Wilson he would have said: 'The Devil the vulgar herd ne'er scent, E'n though he have them by the collar.'[15] What really matters, then, is that people must learn to look and see the concrete events taking place in the spiritual world. But when such a thing is most especially necessary, the powers who want to oppose it are also especially strong, and this then leads people to resist what they should be doing.

There is something I beg you to take into account here in Zurich in connection with your most praiseworthy plan that can be greeted with joy, namely, your plan to bring spiritual science to certain circles who are as yet very negative towards it. What I beg you is that you will not entertain any illusions about this! Much disappointment, indeed initially nothing but disappointment, is what one must expect when one tries to begin in the right way to do things that must be done and have to be done. Nothing must ever prevent us from doing these things. We must be so filled with the impulse, which is the necessary impulse for the present time, that we do what has to be done regardless of whether the consequences, in this instance too, lead more in the one direction or more in the other.

This is the only attitude that can lead to any success. Often what one achieves in one direction is not at all what one intended. I must beg you to realize that one must do far more than seems necessary for the degree of success achieved. This is because making propaganda for spiritual science involves getting involved in something quite different from what is entailed in all the other propagandas put out today in other fields. In other fields one is, after all, usually telling people about things that they already know as thoroughly as the worshippers praying in church know about what the pastor is telling them from the pulpit. Most associations have programmes that are easily assimilated by people. Usually they remain in the realm of abstraction—beautiful programmes that have nothing to do with reality and cannot lead to anything real.

To nurture the endeavours of spiritual life in the fifth post-Atlantean age one must regard them as something that is alive. But look at living creatures, and you will see that spiritual life has a mirror image in natural life. Do the fish in the ocean refrain from laying countless eggs that will perish? Consider how many fish eggs actually turn into fish. Myriads perish! This is how things are in life, and it is also how things are in the spiritual life.

For years and years you can speak again and again to huge crowds, but you must be satisfied if amongst all those huge crowds just a few individuals are touched with enthusiasm, for that is how things are in the living world. We can really only achieve something by imitating nature, which is the mirror image of the spirit. What would happen if nature, having noticed how many eggs perish each year, refrained from allowing all the eggs that perish to be laid in the first place? The process of nature is unceasing, and it is this that leads to evolution. It is not important to consider whether one thing or another can be achieved, whether one person or another has a positive response. What is important is that we regard the matter in hand itself as the impulse and that we cannot help but bring this impulse out into the world.

The reasons, a number of which we have considered in our souls again today, the reasons why one must bring this impulse out into the world of the fifth post-Atlantean age are truly grave enough. And resistance against efforts to do it will be greatest when the need to do it is at its most pressing. As regards the things that happen here on the physical plane, which are just now barbarous indeed, people will have to make the effort to see all these things in conjunction with events that are taking place behind the scenes. Only then will it all become comprehensible.

Today's historians, sociologists, economists and politicians who derive their rules and laws solely from the physical plane—in comparison with what is really needed today, such people are like someone who, when faced with an onerous task, begins to tackle it by lying down and going to sleep on a couch, thinking that he will manage to do the job in his dreams. This is indeed in most cases how those belonging to the life of culture and the life of the various scientific disciplines set about their work. These are people dreaming their way through reality. How do people now write about history, how do they write about sociology? They write as people do who have no idea about the real forces that lie behind the things they dream about. The source of events as drastic as those taking place in our time surrounds the people who are today concerned with science like a room surrounds someone who has never seen it because he has been brought into it while asleep and then goes on sleeping, thus only getting to know the room in his sleep. This is the way in which purely materialistic science gets to know the world.

What I have called Imaginative consciousness in my book *The Riddle of Man*[16] is something that must to some degree come to the humanity of the fifth post-Atlantean age as a matter of course, for certain secrets must come to light because otherwise they will be spread about amongst people in the wrong way by means such as I have told you of today. As I have said, it is not easy to point these things out at the present time, but it is a necessary duty to do so. For in many matters one needs to develop a gift of observation that is different from the coarse gift of observation people have these days.

There are two points I should like to make in connection with what I have been saying. Firstly, people do make some progress today when they endeavour to look at things they would otherwise have regarded as coincidences but instead of doing this now take them so seriously that they perceive them as suggestions for a deepening of the soul. Suppose you read of a particular person having died at a specific place and at a specific time. A number of things will suggest themselves to you if you ask yourself what would have happened if that person had died three months earlier or three months later. This is, of course, merely a question concerning supposed possibilities. But if you ask yourself such a question you can be sure that it can awaken forces in you through which you will reach different insights. Or perhaps you are travelling on a train and have a very important conversation with someone, a conversation that means a great deal to you; or something similar. A materialist will of course regard such things as pure coincidence. But someone who wants to find his way gradually into being able to look behind the scenery of existence, such a person will pay attention to such things. He will ponder these things, not by forcing them into conceptual forms but by sensing the feelings they generate. He will concern himself with these things because they are like hints of the forces at play between things that happen, forces that are more than merely mechanical or mathematical. That was the first point.

The second, which I want to keep on and on mentioning, is that despite today's materialism much that is spiritual is being revealed to human beings. But people are embarrassed to say too much about spiritual experiences they may be having. When someone opens up a little and begins to tell you things because he has developed trust in you, you will hear about how one person did this or another did that. If a person tells you really honestly and candidly why he founded this newspaper or why he did something else, he is telling you a dream, something like a dream; he is describing these things as suggestions coming from the spiritual world. You will find this happening everywhere, much more than you would imagine. Many more things are put into practice out of spiritual impulses than you would think. Only people are embarrassed to admit to this because others do not take them seriously if they talk about such things.

So it is good to deepen your soul's attention in both these directions: firstly to watch closely when something happens that attracts your attention, for this might be a hint coming from somewhere; and secondly to notice how things are revealed to people out of the spiritual world, either in a good or a bad sense, things which give them the impulse to take action in some way. This happens nowadays more than one would imagine.

These are the matters I wanted to draw to your attention today. Next Tuesday we shall talk further about them.

4. *Behind the Scenes of External Events, II*

In the lecture I gave here a week ago[1] I wanted to broach a subject that so much needs to be discussed, a subject that the present tragic events in human life are forcing us to face, a subject that could be defined briefly with the words: Humanity urgently needs to find its way once more to knowledge and awareness of how what takes place here in the world on the physical plane is linked with a concrete spiritual world. Humanity urgently needs to become aware that a spiritual world is working down into every detail of existence in the physical world.

It has to be said that especially in our time one must be aware of the need for consciousness of this to spread amongst humanity. As regards external physical appearance, present-day people are not very different from the human beings who lived in the past ages about which history is ordinarily concerned. (Ordinary historical research does not really go back further than at most about the third post-Atlantean age. What preceded that is only vaguely described by historians, but these vague descriptions are the only ones which people today are prepared to consider.) However, in their soul life human beings have changed a very great deal over the course of time since then, even though it cannot be said that external, physical life or the physical organism has changed all that much. So people do not notice, or are not eager to notice, what is actually happening, what is going on out of impulses coming from the spiritual world.

In fact, we are living in momentous times. By this I am not referring to the silly remark usually clothed in the words: We are living in a time of transition. Of course we are, for every time is a time of transition. But the important thing is to know what it is that is making a transition.

Whatever it is that is making a transition in our time, whatever is taking on new forms and undergoing important transformations, this is something of which we become aware when we are able to turn our attention not only to the lives of beings and creatures who go about here on the earth in physical bodies, but also to beings who do not belong to the physical world, including, of course, human beings who have died. In the world that human beings pass through between death and a new birth one can notice great transformations, and those taking place just now are profoundly far-reaching. But people today are not at all eager to give serious consideration to matters of the spiritual world. And the fact that they do not take this at all seriously can lead for us to very special feelings when we think of how what we call anthroposophy is coming into being.

In order to want to represent the ideas that are put forward by the anthroposophical movement there is no need to feel any particular preference for them. This is different in other movements — and how many movements there are, and associations as well, all of which are convinced that what they want to present to the world is the most essential and necessary thing! The people in all those associations and movements are subjectively fanatical about their movement. They are prejudiced in favour of their programme and they consider their programme to be the source of great bliss and an absolute necessity.

But there is no need to be prejudiced in this way in favour of the anthroposophical movement, for the impulse to represent it can derive from something quite different. To put it briefly (which is so often necessary for us because we can have so little time together) I would say it like this. Having become convinced of the truth of anthroposophical ideas, what then impels us to do all we can to spread the ideas is our sympathy for the people of today who need these ideas, and these people are, actually, almost all those whom we meet. We are impelled by our sympathy for people who must have these ideas and who are doomed to take terrible things upon themselves if they do not have them.

Last time I endeavoured to give you a picture of how things that are incomprehensible on the physical plane become comprehensible when they can be explained in the context of the spiritual world. Today I want to bring forward a number of other important points which at first sight will appear to come from quite another direction. So let us begin with something we encounter wherever we go. In many quarters, though, it is regarded as a sign of especial religious enlightenment if one rejects ideas such as those which we have about what is encountered as soon as one steps across the threshold to the spiritual world, namely, that there one is involved with many spiritual beings, with whole hierarchies of spiritual beings, Angeloi, Archangeloi and so on upwards. Instead it is regarded as a sign of special religious enlightenment if one merely reflects on what is called the One God with whom one seeks to have as intimate and as direct a relationship as possible. This is regarded as the only possible monotheism, and some people are horrified to be told about teachings that speak of a multiplicity of spiritual beings.

Let us be clear about what this means. When a person's only relationship with the spiritual world is the one that is regarded today in religious circles as the usual one, the one cultivated by a Church that fancies itself as enlightened, then that person only has a specific relationship with the spiritual world, a relationship which, although it is one of feeling, only concerns the protecting Angelos, the angel-being with whom he does have a real relationship. And such a person then refers to that angel-being, the only being he can relate to and have certain feelings for, as his god. If he is a Christian he calls this angel-being Christ. He mistakes the angel-being for Christ. It is perhaps difficult to imagine this, but it is so. Protestant theologians who fancy themselves to be enlightened warn strongly against polytheism so that people should gain a direct relationship with the one being, Christ. But however much they talk to people about Christ, what they are saying about Christ refers solely to the individual's relationship with his own angel-being. Thus in our time monotheism is in danger of becoming the worship by each human being of his own individual angel.

There is much that people do not yet want to admit even though it lives among them as a reality. The objective observer, meanwhile, can see how they are beginning to develop all kinds of rather disastrous ideas and feelings out of such illusions. Because people each pray to their own angel they each have their own god, while erroneously believing that they share their god with the others. In fact the monotheists of today each pray only to their own angel, but as the words resound together which each is speaking to his own angel in an egoistic relationship with his own angel-being, they think that they are talking of a god whom they all share. If this were to develop further, people as individual human beings would begin to develop more and more what we already see nations manifesting in a terrible way. Although still speaking theoretically of the One God, they do not seriously want to recognize this divinity, especially now, for each nation wants to have its own god.

This is what comes to the fore in a general way. In reality every human being today wants to have his own god, and so he uses the term monotheism for the relationship he has with only his own Angelos-being. Since all relationships are dulled in a time when the aim is to develop abilities to see solely what is sense-perceptible, people do not notice that things are as I have just described them. In speaking about concrete relationships between human beings and the spiritual world to people who have not as yet taken note of any anthroposophical concepts, we find everywhere that they do not want to go into such things. They shy away from entering into this subject. They do not want to muster the courage to connect their thoughts with impulses that are said to come from the spiritual world. Something like this has always been the case in times of crisis, and we are now living in a time of crisis. With exceedingly painful feelings we have to observe how inattentive today's humanity is as regards the tragic events of the present time which speak so eloquently and clearly, how disinclined people are to pay proper attention to the events of the present time apart from being forced to take note of the material circumstances. People really do have to be forced to notice that what is going on during these years is everywhere presenting human souls with profoundly incisive impulses for humanity.

This is why people have not listened when they have been shown, by whatever means, that important, decisive things must be thought and done by today's humanity in order to extricate itself from the miseries of the present time, and that the things that have to be thought and done must be born out of spiritual knowledge, out of concrete spiritual facts. Constantly emphasizing the spiritual in a general way while going on and on about how human beings should deepen themselves spiritually and so on — none of this leads anywhere. What matters is that the people of today must win through to concrete relationships with the spiritual world. For us it is understandable that in earlier ages, when they had stronger connections with the spiritual world, people's attention was drawn to those concrete connections whereas nowadays these are no longer comprehended. In earlier ages people did not yet indulge in generalized chatter about humanity milling around down here on the earth while something divine hovered about up above; people then talked in concrete terms.

The most beautiful and meaningful outpourings of such concrete relationships are to be found in prophecies such as those of Daniel or of the Book of Revelation which do not merely state: 'You human beings, you must put your trust in One God, you must believe in One God.' Those writings tell of one kingdom, a second kingdom, a third kingdom and how such kingdoms must follow one after the other, and they tell in concrete ways of the relationship of the spiritual world with the physical, sense-perceptible earth. But humanity today has completely lost the habit of speaking in such concrete ways about the relationship between the spiritual and the physical.

Humanity today wants to apply the same yardstick to everything and invent theories according to which people all over the globe may be awarded the same standard of earthly happiness. Today's socialist thinks that certain ideas apply equally to human life in England, America, Russia or Asia. If every state were to arrange its affairs as socialism prescribes then the happiness which people everywhere dream about would automatically ensue. That is what people think.

But these are abstractions, unreal concepts and ideas. Not knowing that one thing is prepared in one location on the earth by one particular people while another is prepared at another location, not having the ability to comprehend the great difference between West and East: this is what must cause endless confusion and endless chaos. Only those who can build a bridge from their soul to the objective facts can work in a beneficial way to shape earthly existence.

But people do not want to build this bridge. Again and again just now, an inner necessity compels me to speak to our friends in various places about a certain event that took place during the final third of the nineteenth century, one that is significant and deeply incisive for human evolution, an event known to all the various occult schools, although they are often not able to give a correct account of how the event ran its course.

Today once again I want to mention briefly what it is about. From the year 1841 onwards a battle of spirits took place in spiritual realms between certain beings of the higher hierarchies and other beings who were above them. The beings who rebelled in the years between 1841 and 1879, and who fought a battle of rebellion during that period, had earlier been employed in a positive way by the wise guides of the universe. Beings who at one time are rebellious and evil and become spirits of darkness are, at other times, beings whose services are used for the good. So I am speaking here of beings who until 1841 were employed by higher beings in the service of the wise guides of the world but who from then onwards had aims that differed from those of the superior beings. These beings fought a significant battle in the spiritual world, one of those battles that take place quite frequently, though at various levels, a battle that in legend is symbolized by the battle of Michael with the dragon.

This battle ended in the autumn of 1879 with certain spirits of darkness being thrown down from the spiritual realms into the realm of the earth, since when they have been at work amongst human beings, entering into their will impulses, entering into their motivations, entering into whatever human beings can grasp in thought, in short, into everything connected with human beings. So certain spirits of darkness have been amongst human beings since the autumn of 1879, and people must become aware of them if they are to understand earthly events. It is entirely correct to say that because these beings were thrown out in 1879 the heavens are now free of them while the earth is full of them.

The best way of describing what these beings wanted to achieve by means of their battle of rebellion from 1841 to 1879[2] is to say that they wanted to prevent the spiritual wisdom that must necessarily be revealed to human beings from the twentieth century onwards from entering into human souls. They wanted to retain the spiritual wisdom within the spiritual world and not let it enter into human souls. The only way of ensuring that the human sense for spiritual knowledge would be opened up from the twentieth century onwards was to remove the impeding spirits of darkness from the spiritual realm so that the spiritual knowledge destined for human beings could come down. But now that those spirits of darkness are moving about amongst human beings here on earth, they are once again working to confuse people. Their aim now is to make sure that people fail to enter into the right relationship with the spiritual truths, so that the healing purpose of those truths is kept away from human beings.

The only way of counteracting this is to apply clear recognition and understanding to these matters. But there are certain secret brotherhoods who have made it their task to work for the opposite of this. They want to have the wisdom only within their closest circle so that they can use it in the service of their own lust for power. This is the battle we are now fighting. On the one hand there is the need to guide humanity in the right way by letting people take in the spiritual wisdom. On the other there are the closed secret brotherhoods of a nasty kind whose very aim is *not* to let the wisdom enter into humanity, so that people will remain stupid and foolish as far as the spiritual world is concerned while those within the closely guarded brotherhoods carry on their machinations from there.

The events of the present time are full of whole bundles of these machinations, and it will be especially calamitous for humanity if people fail to recognize that such machinations are at work. You will feel as though a kind of light has been turned on regarding what is happening behind these matters when I tell you of certain truths, truths that, like ripe plums dropping from a tree, are meant to drop down out of the spiritual world into the human realm but are being prevented from spreading also because people have presuppositions and misconceptions about them and are afraid of them.

I would like to speak about this in terms that are as concrete as possible. Important, significant consequences arise out of the fact that a number of spirits of darkness were thrown out in 1879 and have since dwelt in the human realm. The main consequence of this fact is that since then thinking, clear thinking, has become immeasurably more important for human beings than was formerly the case. Never before has there been a time when clear thinking has been as necessary for human evolution as are eating and drinking for the preservation of the physical body. For if people think without clarity now in our time and on into the future, they will not be able to see in the right light those ripe truths that are to drop down from the spiritual world. Above all they will not understand the great and profound significance for the whole of human evolution of the Mystery of Golgotha, the appearance of Christ within the evolution of humanity. Many people talk about Christ Jesus. But to talk about the profound significance accorded to the whole of human evolution on the earth by the Mystery of Golgotha, this is something that today's theology actually wants to prevent. There has of course only been a slow and gradual development of what is going to come about through the Mystery of Golgotha, and it will only come to the fore in its full intensity during our present century.

In olden times there still existed faculties inherited from the ages when human beings had an atavistic inner life filled with spirituality. Only in our age has it become necessary for people to work at achieving spirituality if this is what they want to have. That is why certain quite specific manifestations are arising in our time, in fact from 1879 onwards. Because our outer vision has become so coarse, we can only see these things clearly when we look with the eyes of our soul into the realm which human beings enter after stepping through the gate of death. There we see that the manner in which souls born prior to 1879 re-enter the spiritual world after death is different from how all those souls will arrive back who have been born since 1879. This is a profoundly incisive event.

This profoundly incisive event has the effect, especially, that in their souls human beings become increasingly similar to their thoughts, to what they regard as their understanding of things. This may be a strange truth for the people of today, but it is a truth nevertheless. It is important and essential to see certain things in the right light, with clear thoughts, with valid thoughts, with thoughts imbued through and through with reality. To see Darwinism correctly, for example as I endeavoured to present it yesterday in the public lecture,[3] this is good. But to see it as the basis for the only valid view of the world, to see it as meaning that only one thing is correct, namely, that the human being is descended from the animals, to have the living thought about oneself 'I am descended from the animals, I have originated only out of the same forces that also form the animals' — all this leads souls nowadays to resemble their own inner pictures.

It is important to know this! When a soul like this has laid aside its body it undergoes the misfortune of having to see itself as resembling its own inner pictures. Those who believe while in the physical body that only animal forces have played a part in their development are building for themselves a consciousness after death with which they will have to perceive themselves as animals. For now that the event of 1879 has properly brought to fulfilment the character of the fifth post-Atlantean age, the thoughts which human beings make for themselves serve to make human souls become transformed into these thoughts.

That is why I said earlier that there is no need to have any particular preference for the spiritual science of anthroposophy in order to want to represent it. All one needs is sympathy with those who use such thoughts: these thoughts are creative thoughts in the life of the soul because human beings are destined in the future to become what they regard themselves to be. This is something that had to come about during the course of wisely guided world evolution so that the human being might really attain to a full and free consciousness of self. One aspect is that the gods had to give the human being the possibility of becoming his own creation. The other aspect is that in order for the human being to be able to give this self-created being a supersensible purpose, in order for him to be able to find in what he has made of himself something that can give him an eternal direction for the future—for this it was that Christ Jesus entered into the Mystery of Golgotha. If one understands Christ Jesus through spiritual science, if one understands him in one's thoughts, then one can find the way to him: the way from the animal nature to the divine.

This truth becomes especially evident to those who can look with the eyes of the soul into the realm which human beings enter after death. Those born before 1879 still take a certain remnant back with them which protects them from becoming only what they were able to imagine while here on earth. And indeed for some time to come people will still be protected from becoming what they have imagined themselves to be—for these things only come into effect gradually. But, paradoxically, this protection will only be made possible through suffering, it will only be possible if they can take upon themselves the suffering of knowledge by which they themselves sense the unsatisfactory nature of their ideas about the human being. Harmony with oneself coupled with knowledge that allows the human being to be human after death, this will only come about in the future if human beings become aware, while they are here in the physical body, of their true connections with the spiritual world.

Those whose materialistic ideas still make them reject concrete spiritual knowledge today will take a long time before being able to accept that the year 1879 brought with it this kind of change. Yet it is necessary for such knowledge to be accepted. So you see how important it is, and how much more important it will become in the future, that the spiritual knowledge available should be allowed to spread throughout the earth. But, meanwhile, in order to promote their affairs the spirits of darkness will place especial emphasis on creating confusion amongst human beings so that they fail to form the right thoughts into which they will be transformed after death.

The human being has to become what he thinks himself to be. This is a truth that was destined to become known by human beings from the time in the nineteenth century onwards when those important changes came about. Human beings must will to be what they can in reality be, they must be able to think about their being if they are to be that being in their soul. Even today those who have died will be able to announce as a rightful mature truth: 'The soul is what it is able to think itself to be.' Yet since the time when it has become necessary to spread the truth 'The soul is what it is able to think itself to be', since that time the spirits of darkness have managed to inspire into people what they represent as the truth, which is: 'The human being is what he eats'.[4]

Although the maxim 'The human being is what he eats' is not recognized theoretically amongst the broader population, nevertheless people live their lives in practice as though they do agree that the human being really is nothing more than what he eats. In fact, life as it is lived in practice is aiming more and more to bring this to the fore in outer life as well. More than anyone might believe, very much more than anyone might believe, the sad and tragic events of the present time have arisen as a consequence of the principle 'The human being is what he eats'. In a far more profound sense than is realized by today's superficial way of thinking, it is these very lowly things that are causing so much blood to flow. Humanity has indeed been inoculated with the sentence: 'The human being is what he eats'. And many battles are being fought about matters that are connected with such things.

Especially for this reason it is so necessary for thoughts that are fitting for our age to be spread about. Thought will gradually have to be recognized as a real soul force rather than the pitiable abstraction which modern times have turned it into and are now so proud of as well. In bygone ages there was still an ancient heritage that linked humanity with the spiritual world. But although that atavistic clairvoyance more or less vanished many centuries ago, the ancient heritage has still been present in the feeling and the will. But now the time has come when what is conscious must come more and more to the fore as a real force, and that is why in our time the spirits of opposition, the spirits of darkness are rushing to the attack in order to counteract genuine thought with abstract thoughts in the form of all kinds of world programmes. The connection between these things must be clearly seen. People must understand that the thought as such must become more and more real.

There are still today so many people who say: 'Well, we shall see what comes after death, we'll find out about it all in good time. But there's no need to bother about it just now while we serve life. Once we enter that other world over there we'll see quite clearly what it is like.' In fact, if the one thing is true, namely, that over there we are what we have here imagined about ourselves, then there is also something else that is true. Consider a thought that is not at all rare today when someone has died and left relatives behind. If the latter are perhaps not without thoughts although tending to be materialistic, they cannot help having the thought that their dead relative is decaying in the grave or that they still have what remains of him collected up in an urn, or suchlike. Well, so long as people are without thoughts they can be materialists and yet not have this belief. But if materialism triumphs, then people will increasingly believe: All that is left of the dead person is decaying in the urn or in the grave. This thought is a real force. It is an untruth. If those left behind think that the dead person is no longer alive and that he is no longer here, then this is an erroneous thought, but this erroneous thought is nevertheless real and actual in the souls of the people who think it. And the dead person perceives this real thought; he perceives it as something very significant for himself. It is not unimportant, but in fact profoundly important, if those who remain behind here cultivate in their living inner soul life the thought of the dead person continuing to live in the spiritual world, or if they merely give way to the lament: 'He's dead, that's all, he is decaying.' These two things are not equally valid for they are actually very essentially different.

It is now scarcely possible to be here in Zurich without everywhere coming up against what people call analytical psychology, psychoanalysis, which is now being carried on everywhere but especially strongly here.[5] These psycho-analysts, it must be said, are now beginning to pay attention to matters of spirit and soul; they are beginning to think about spirit and soul because they are being so strongly confronted with this element. I would here like to describe in a few words one particular feature of this psychoanalysis.

Think of someone who suffers from hysterical symptoms. Hysterical symptoms are being especially noticed now because of the form they take these days. In any age close attention is paid to those disorders that manifest particularly strongly in that age; people seek to find where the causes might lie. Well, psychoanalysis has now reached the point where it is saying that these hysterical symptoms which manifest so frequently have their causes in the soul. It cannot find the causes in the material realm, in the physiological or biological element, so they must lie in the soul realm. The favoured place for seeking all kinds of causes for various hysterical symptoms lies, at present, in the subconscious soul realm. They say: 'Here is someone who manifests hysterical symptoms; they arise because what is at work in him lies not in his consciousness but beneath the threshold of his consciousness whence it keeps rising up like a subterranean wave, a "subsoulian" wave.'

This is the beginning of a dangerous game. The psychoanalysts search for all kinds of isolated, subterranean, hidden soul provinces, as they call it. In someone who is 30 years old they look for aberrations in his seventh year which were not lived through fully at that time; these must be brought back into his consciousness because bringing things back into consciousness is supposed to heal, and so on. This is a game with extremely dangerous weapons! Out on the physical battlefield people are today fighting with very dangerous weapons. But here in many fields a game is being played with weapons of knowledge that are no less dangerous because people lack the will to deepen their knowledge through spiritual science in order to reach a real understanding of the symptoms that rise up before their souls. They tackle the matter with inadequate tools of knowledge, and that is a dangerous game.

It is perfectly true to say that subconscious elements which fail to rise up into consciousness do play a part in many people nowadays. But what the psychoanalysts imagine they have found is as a rule the very least significant part, and that is why their successes in healing patients are on the whole rather questionable. When you find that a woman of 30 underwent some sort of sexual aberration in her fourteenth year which was not fully lived through so that the consequences continue to grow wildly and cause hysteria, what you have actually discovered is the most inconsequential aspect of the matter. In one case or another what you discover might in fact be quite correct, but it will lead to even greater misunderstanding if its full import is not understood.

One thing above all, though, is certainly true, and that is that countless subconscious elements do indeed haunt human beings today, and they are much harrassed by these; and the diseases of civilization are caused by them.

What is this? Consider what I have already said. The thought of the dead person who is no longer here lives in the soul; it lives somehow, without the soul thinking about it much; it lives only because the soul is today still without thought, and the soul is rather sensitive with regard to such thoughtless thoughts. When this happens the dead person is forced by eternal universal laws to live with this thought; the dead person haunts the soul of the living person who has remained behind.

The only way to counteract this is by knowing that the dead person lives. People on the physical plane will be more and more driven into soul illnesses by their lack of belief that the dead are alive. As a rule it is not youthful sexual aberrations that bring about these diseases, but thoughts that do not believe. For in our time thoughts are called upon to become real forces. They are called upon to become real forces, but not only forces that work for themselves; they work for themselves when after death the soul increasingly resembles what it imagined itself to be while it was in the body. But these thoughts become real forces in a higher sense as well in that they even bind beings, in this case those who have died, in a wrong way to those who are still alive.

The only way to counteract this is by maintaining as far as one can a connection with the one who has died in that one regards him as continuing to live. This saves the relationship with the dead person from becoming a disaster not only for oneself who has remained behind but also in some ways for the dead person who is necessitated by an eternal, wisdom-filled law to haunt the one who has remained behind in a way that does not come to the consciousness of that person but manifests purely in symptoms of disease.

So what is the real remedy for many of the symptoms which psychoanalysts are encountering today? The remedy is to spread knowledge about the spiritual world. This is the universal remedy, the universal therapy, and not those individual treatments that are bestowed upon individual patients.

So you see, life is calling on us not to think that while we are here we should pay attention only to physical life while imagining that when we step through the gate of death it will be soon enough to find out what kind of a world we shall discover there. For it is a fact that just as our life here is important for the life we shall enter between death and a new birth, so is the life of souls between death and a new birth important for the souls here.

What I have been telling you is a thought, the thought of disbelieving the existence of those who have died. But the dead are, and should be, linked to the living by many bonds; and what I have been speaking about is only one of those bonds. There are also many other legitimate bonds which are needed to bring about the proper connections with the spiritual world. Spiritual science, the spiritual science of anthroposophy, searches for the right connections. The life human beings lead with one another here on the earth will only follow a correct course if people here on the earth enter into a proper relationship with the spiritual world. Otherwise it will become more and more possible for individuals to become presumptuous and embark on machinations such as those I spoke of last Tuesday, in order to gain power over others.[6]

There is one thing, especially, about which we must be clear: When we look towards the East where just now the events that are happening are very intensive signs of something, we shall only gain an understanding of this if we gain inward clarity about the nature of what is there in the East. Look at what we have been saying for years about the inclinations of the eastern peoples in relation to the sixth post-Atlantean cultural age.[7] This will bring clarity about all that is so confusing which has to come from the East because out of what is happening there now something quite different must develop, something it will not be easy to be so complacent about. The important thing to do is to find an entry in the right way into all those streams that are appearing just now and will continue to appear even more in the future. And the right entry can be found by pressing forward to knowledge about the spiritual world that can be discovered in the right way through spiritual science. In this way, too, the right relationship with the spiritual world can be found.

Last time I drew your attention to a wrong relationship

with the spiritual world which is being sought in a particular quarter.[8] I told you that quite specific machinations were being used to dispatch people away from life here and up into the spiritual world in such a way that their life here had not been fully lived so that they could still make use of certain forces once they had entered into the world in which we live between death and a new birth. Then certain unscrupulous brotherhoods who only want to satisfy their own lust for power can use mediums in order to bring into the world some specific knowledge that can come from those who have died once they have been given the possibility of acquiring such knowledge.

These secret brotherhoods are, as a rule, also the ones that mislead people with regard to the most important matters to do with the spiritual world. I have told you that in November 1879 an important event took place, a battle between the forces of darkness and the forces of light of which the outcome is depicted in the image of Michael and the dragon. What is important about this, however, is not the fact that I have told you about it, for this was an event that had to happen, an event that was predestined in world evolution about which you can read in many different books, so that it is a truth that is not at all esoteric. The important thing is that I endeavour to make clear to you the true significance of what actually happened and also the proper way in which human beings should relate to this event. That is what is important. The fact that this event was coming was known to Eliphas Levi, to Baader, to Saint-Martin, all of whom wrote about it.[9] There is nothing at all esoteric about it. But in our time there are ongoing efforts to create confusion about such events in people's heads, perhaps so much confusion that human heads take such things to be nothing but superstition and not real even though knowledge about them has already been put about by older scholars who are in the know. That is why it is important to be given appropriate concepts about these things.

Today there is a proper path along which one can approach the spiritual truths that have been seeping down into the physical world from the spiritual world. This proper path is the one shown by spiritual science. And if the stream of this spiritual science does not stray from the pure and genuine will, then it will lead people to a right relationship between the physical world and the spiritual world. But to attain what must be attained and brought to people is a strenuous business requiring effort. The comfortable attitudes people have today will have to be put aside, for effort is required. When one speaks about impulses that work down from the spiritual world and will also play a part in shaping the future it happens repeatedly that people come who want specific information about one thing or another. Such people want to be told, for example, exactly what will come out of the present war in 1920. Such people fail to grasp that it is not permitted to burden the future by elaborating on every detail, but that in spite of this, knowledge about the future can be absolutely certain, effective and certain, and that one must take account of it. It is so very difficult to make people understand this.

Let me use an example to clarify this, since you are likely to say: 'What does he mean? On the one hand he tells us that details are harmful to knowledge of the future, and on the other hand he says one should listen carefully to this knowledge about the future because it brings forward true things about the future.'

I want to use a really simple example to show you what I mean. Imagine a bad and a good chess player. A bad chess player will make bad moves, he will not do any good and will lose the game. A good player will have more opportunities and will win the game. The bad chess player simply makes wrong moves while the good one makes the right moves at the right time. But does the good player waste his thoughts on working out in detail what moves his opponent might make later on? As a good player must he know now what moves his opponent will make in two hours? No, there is no need for him to know this! Yet even without this knowledge his art of playing chess correctly and well does not remain without effect. When the future comes he will do the right thing because he has insight into what the right moves are, but he will do the wrong thing if he has no insight into what the right moves are. He cannot avoid facing up to the free will of his opponent. So you cannot ask: 'What is the use of being able to play chess properly if the opponent is present?' In fact there is a great deal of use in being able to play chess properly. If you think more profoundly about this comparison I am sure you will discover what I mean.

This comparison will also show you the relevance of what anyone who is knowledgeable about esoteric matters will tell you: that as soon as you derive the impulses for your actions in the physical world out of the spiritual world you must at that same moment be prepared to be confronted by other spiritual powers, that you will have opponents with whom you will have to reckon, that there will be no free space where you can put everything into action. This is what is uncomfortable in these things. Get to know esoteric impulses, impulses that have been called down from the spiritual world and then try, perhaps as a politician, to put them into practice. If you are a true contemporary of the present age you will much prefer it if everything runs smoothly, if these impulses simply flow in while you regulate everything. But if you have effective spiritual impulses, especially esoteric impulses, which you want to apply in the physical world you will everywhere have to reckon not only with the free will of people in this world but also of higher beings. So as things stand today you cannot reckon with finding a free space in front of you; you will have to realize that you will be working in a space that is already well filled.

So the important thing is to get to know, through a genuine spiritual science, the right things for example about the nature of the sixth post-Atlantean cultural age, which is being prepared over in the East, and then to carry out the right esoteric impulse in each individual situation, just as the chess player makes his moves according to the moves of his opponent. The important thing really is that one must learn to find a living entry into the spiritual world and then do the right thing in each individual case. It is not simply overall abstract programmes that are important but a heightening of one's spiritual vitality, a continuous exercising of effort.

People want abstract programmes nowadays, they want to hear stated in five sentences what should be done all over the world; they want delegates to be sent from every state on earth who will meet in a world tribunal and vote on everything that is to happen all over the earth in accordance with an accepted norm. Yet the important thing to realize is that knowledge of the spiritual world is what is required of human beings, a continuous effort to make contact with the spiritual world.

This, though, is linked with something else. It is linked with the fact that one has to reckon with the forces that are one's opponents and cannot simply rely on one's own powers; the opponents have to be reckoned with. But this has nothing to do with the idea of power. Impulses brought down from the esoteric world will be the right ones and will bring about what is right; and it will never be possible to use them in the service of power as such. That is impossible.

What must one do if one wants to work in the service of power factors as such? One must try to gain knowledge about the future in an improper way as I described last time: by dispatching people through death in a manner that enables them to retain the use of earthly forces and then getting them to impart what is to happen through mediums. In this way certain secret brotherhoods have gained some portions of knowledge about the relationship of the West to the East, and all kinds of machinations have been set in train which are functioning in accordance with that knowledge. For knowledge that is placed at the disposal of the lust for power seeks to attain something entirely specific.

The honest, proper acquisition of esoteric impulses only puts into practice what takes account also of the Angelos-being of each individual living person. One knows that every individual with regard to whom one is using esoteric impulses is also a soul who has a relationship with the spiritual world; one regards such a one as a living being. The way in which the West ought to be treating the East should everywhere involve being open to the possibility of reckoning with the living partners, the angels who protect each individual human being.

But this is irksome! Those others want to get rid of this influence by means of ahrimanic powers, so that power alone can hold sway on this side; but such a thing can only be brought about by gaining possession of the impulses for the future in the wrong way as I described last time. Our age is suffering immensely from the way impulses gained in the manner described are playing a part in the events that happen. The whole task of those who seek the truth in an honest way today involves in the first place the duty to convince oneself that impulses in the bad sense do exist, and to convince oneself that the only way to work into the future in the right way is through finding the right impulses in the proper way by the path of spiritual science.

Dear friends, you can see from this that to serve spiritual science is not a one-sided matter, for it is a service rendered by both the living and the dead. It is an earnest matter. What I wanted to do just now, when our friends here in Zurich are preparing to bring spiritual science into suitable circles, was to speak within our Society here about these earnest matters of spiritual knowledge in recent and present times. It is noticeable even within our Society how various opposing powers are at work. Only consider what has been going on, roughly since this war began, by way of defamations and accusations of the will which I and others are experiencing. In this, too, opposing powers are obviously playing their part.[10]

From the way we have been speaking during these considerations it will have become clear to you that our time needs a renewal of its spiritual life, and that it needs people to wake up from a kind of sleeping state. Again and again we meet people who think: 'Well, now there is a war, but after that peace will come and then the matter will be done with.' But this is not how things are. The things that are happening today are significant signs. But they are incomprehensible to anyone who does not want to deepen his soul life through spiritual science. And because the times are so serious, because it will become more and more difficult to fight even the kind of battle our friends here have fought in order to make such functions as this one possible,

I want to mention this circumstance especially, and in this case also with my utmost gratitude. I want to mention it with gratitude on the one hand out of the mood of spiritual science, and on the other because our dear friends here in Zurich have taken up the battle against unfavourable circumstances so kindly and with such energy and have not spared themselves any effort to make these lectures possible under these very unfavourable circumstances. So the fine aim these Zurich friends set themselves has been realized even though it will become increasingly difficult to organize such events owing to the increasing resistance of these times.

I especially want to mention the fact that these difficulties will continue to increase more and more. So we must realize that we shall have to make the best use in the near future of the time we can still fight for in which to put on our lectures, and that is why I wanted to express these thanks to our dear Zurich friends who have made the greatest efforts to enable both the public and the branch lectures to take place.[11] Later, when we look back over these things, we will surely realize how significant it is that we have been able to be together and speak together in this way just at the present time when such tragic events are taking place in the world.

So let us continue to work in the sense of the spiritual-scientific impulse, and endeavour to do whatever can be wrested from the difficult circumstances of this time in the conviction, which can arise in us out of a true understanding of spiritual science, that in the great stream of today's tragic and devastating events we are doing something very important and incisive for this age. What we are doing is something that is flowing into the stream of events. That this is happening may not be very obvious just now, but it is significant nonetheless. If this thought can imbue us then it will give us the strength to carry on; this thought will have the strength within it to send out beams into our time in the right way. Such thoughts must be absorbed and accepted by our time. Let us live in this conviction as though in an atmosphere of spirit! It can come to us out of spiritual science if we understand this spiritual science in the right way.

Let us remain together in this sense, my dear friends.

Dornach, 18 November 1917

5. Individual Spirit Beings and the Constant Foundation of the Universe, I

You will remember our considerations regarding various claims and assertions made nowadays by psychoanalysts.[1] My intention was to show that the concept of the unconscious as defined by psychoanalysis lacks foundation. So long as psychoanalysts cannot get beyond this totally negative concept of the unconscious we shall have to stand by our statement that psychoanalysis is using inadequate tools for its work on a phenomenon which it is important to work on today. Nevertheless, since the psychoanalysts do indeed endeavour to research the spirit-soul element and also follow up this spirit-soul element in the social realm, one cannot but grant that their efforts represent a more significant effort than that achieved in this realm by official academic science. However, since efforts are also under way to bring analytical psychology into everyday life through education, through therapy and soon probably also through social politics, the dangers involved must give rise to some concern.

So let us ask: What is it that today's researchers are unable but also unwilling to get to grips with? They recognize that there is a soul element which lies outside consciousness; indeed they seek to find the soul element that is outside consciousness. But they cannot make the effort to recognize the spirit itself. Spirit can never in any way be encompassed by the concept of the unconscious, for an unconscious spirit would be like a human being without a head. I have pointed out to you that in certain states of hysteria there are people who can go about in the street and see only the body but not the head of other people.[2] Not seeing anyone's head is a specific kind of illness. Similarly, amongst today's researchers there are some who think they are seeing the whole spirit. But by presenting it as something unconscious they show that they themselves are victims of the illusion that there would be an unconscious spirit, a spirit without consciousness, if we were to step across the threshold of consciousness either in the right sense, as we always do on the basis of spiritual-scientific research, or in a pathological, abnormal way, which is always the case with patients who are treated by psychoanalysts.

When we step across the threshold of consciousness we always enter a realm of spirit. Whether it is subconscious or superconscious, it is always a realm of spirit, a realm in which the spirit is conscious in one way or another, in one form or another. Where there is spirit there is consciousness. All we have to do is find out what conditions the consciousness is subject to. Spiritual science, in particular, gives us the possibility of recognizing which kind of consciousness a particular form of spirituality has.

Last week we talked of a woman leaving a social gathering and then running away from horses and having to be prevented from jumping into a river before being brought back to the house she had just left in order there to be brought together with the host because she was in love with him in some unclear, subconscious way.[3] It cannot be said in such a case that the spirit of which the woman is not conscious, but which is urging and leading her on, is an

unconscious spirit, nor that it is an unconscious soul element. No, it is something very conscious. The demonic
spirit who leads the woman back to the man whom she
loves in an improper way is actually much cleverer in its
consciousness than is the woman herself in her upper
storey, by which I mean her consciousness.

When we step across the threshold of consciousness in
some way, the spirits who move about there are not
unconscious spirits; they are spirits who are conscious in
the way they move about and get active. The term
'unconscious spirit' as used by psychoanalysts is mean-
ingless. I might just as easily, seeing things from my point of
view, regard this whole illustrious gathering sitting here as
my unconscious if I knew nothing about it. It would be
equally wrong to call the spiritual beings who are around
us—and who in cases like the one mentioned seize hold of
the person—unconcious spirits. They are subconscious,
they are not grasped by the consciousness that happens to
be in us at that moment. But for themselves they are entirely
conscious.

Especially for the task of spiritual science in our time it is
extremely important to know this because knowledge about
the spirit realm that lies beyond the threshold, knowledge
about real individualities who are aware of themselves, is
not something known only to present-day spiritual science,
for it is in fact knowledge that is very ancient indeed. In
earlier times it was known through the old atavistic art of
clairvoyance. But today it is known by other means; one is
gradually learning about it. Knowledge about real spirits
who are outside the scope of human consciousness and
whose conditions of life are not like those of human beings
although they are in constant contact with them and can
seize hold of them in their thinking, feeling and will, *this*

knowledge has always existed. It is knowledge that was always regarded as the secret possession of certain brotherhoods who treated it within their circle as a strictly esoteric matter. Why did they treat it as being strictly esoteric? To enter into an explanation of this now would be going too far, but this much can be said: The individual brotherhoods were always honestly of the opinion that the majority of human beings were insufficiently mature to possess this wisdom. And this was to a large extent indeed the case. But many other brotherhoods, those we call the brotherhoods of the left-hand path,[4] endeavoured to keep this knowledge to themselves also because when such knowledge is possessed by a small group it gives that group power over others who do not possess it. And there have always been endeavours aimed at ensuring that certain groups had power over others. This could be done by regarding certain knowledge as an esoteric matter but then using it to gain power over something else.

Today it is especially necessary to be really clear about these things. As you know, and as I have been telling you in recent lectures,[5] humanity has been living in a very special spiritual situation since 1879. Very specially effective spirits of darkness have been removed from the spiritual world into the physical since 1879, and those who hold the secrets connected with this fact in an unlawful manner within small groups are able to do all kinds of mischief with these things. Today I shall begin by showing you how certain secrets connected with the evolution of the present time can be misused. You must then make an effort to bring together what I shall tell you today, which is more the historical aspect, with what I shall say about it tomorrow.

You all know that for quite a while now within our anthroposophical stream of spiritual science attention has been drawn to the fact that the twentieth century is one in which a special relationship of human evolution with Christ is to come about. In the twentieth century, in fact during the first half, as you know, an event will take place which is also hinted at in the first of my Mystery Plays,[6] namely, that Christ will become for a sufficiently large number of people a being who is actually present in the etheric realm.

We know that we are now living in the age of materialism. We know that materialism has been reaching its zenith since about the middle of the nineteenth century. However, the reality is that opposite poles always coincide. The zenith of materialism in human evolution has to coincide with its opposite, namely, an inwardness in human evolution that leads to Christ being indeed seen in the etheric realm.

It is understandable that this very announcement about the new relationship which Christ is about to enter into with humanity will be met with upset and aversion amongst those who, as members of certain brotherhoods, want to make use of the knowledge of this twentieth-century event, this event of the appearance of the etheric Christ, for their own ends and therefore do not want it to become common knowledge. There are some brotherhoods—and brotherhoods also influence public opinion in ways that people are least likely to notice—there are certain secret brotherhoods who put it about that materialism will soon fizzle out, indeed that it has already fizzled out in some ways.

Those unfortunate, pitiable—'clever' in quotation marks—individuals who spread the doctrine in all kinds of meetings, books and associations that materialism has run its course and that comprehension of the spirit is already beginning to dawn, although they are unable to do more than pronounce the word 'spirit' and dole out a few isolated empty phrases, these are the individuals who are more or less serving those who have an interest in putting about something that is untrue, namely, that materialism has fizzled out. This is an untruth, for materialism is, on the contrary, still on the increase, and it will flourish best when people delude themselves into believing that they are no longer materialists. Materialism is on the increase, and it will continue being on the increase for another four to five hundred years.

As I have so often stressed here, what is needed now is a clear and conscious awareness of the fact that this is the case. Humanity will remain unscathed if human beings work in their spiritual and cultural life in the knowledge that the fifth post-Atlantean epoch has the task of drawing forth from general human evolution what is materialistic in its essence. But at the same time this must be countered with an equal degree of what is spiritual in its essence. In previous lectures[7] I have spoken about what human beings must learn in the fifth post-Atlantean age, namely, to wage a fully conscious battle against the evil that is making its appearance in human evolution. Just as the battle regarding an understanding of birth and death took place during the fourth post-Atlantean age, so is it now time for the battle regarding the understanding of evil. The important thing now is to grasp spiritual teachings in full consciousness, not to throw dust in the eyes of one's contemporaries as though the devil of materialism did not exist. This devil will be very much on the increase. Those who are dealing with these things in a wrong way know about the event of Christ's appearance just as well as I do; but they are treating this event in a different way. To understand why this is one must pay attention to the following.

With humanity as it is in this fifth post-Atlantean age

many people in their indolence utter the entirely unjustified sentence: 'What we have to do while we are living here between birth and death is immerse ourselves fully in life; whether we then enter a spiritual world after passing through death remains to be seen, and meanwhile we can wait. Let us enjoy life as though nothing but a physical world existed. When we step into the spiritual world through death, well, we shall see then whether such a world exists!' This statement is just about as intelligent as the oath: 'As truly as there is a God in heaven, I am an atheist!'[8] The degree of intelligence in that remark is about the same as in this oath; yet it is how many people think who say: 'We shall see after we die what it is like over there; meanwhile there is no need to bother with any kind of spiritual science.'

An attitude of this kind has always been highly questionable, but in our fifth post-Atlantean age it is particularly fatal because it is being especially urged upon human beings now through the dominance of evil. The evolutionary conditions that hold sway at present mean that when human beings pass through the gate of death they take with them the conditions of consciousness which they themselves have created for their own lives between birth and death. Those who under present conditions concern themselves solely with ideas, concepts and feelings relating to the physical, sense-perceptible world are condemning themselves to living after death in surroundings to which only the concepts developed during bodily life refer. Whereas those who absorb spiritual ideas enter into the spiritual world in the right way, those who refuse to absorb spiritual ideas have to remain, in a certain way, within earthly conditions until — and this takes a long time — they have learned over there to absorb spiritual concepts to a degree in which these can carry them over into the spiritual world.

So, our environment over there is determined by whether or not we absorb spiritual concepts here. It has to be said with much pity that many of those who have resisted or been prevented from absorbing spiritual concepts here during life find themselves wandering about on the earth even when they are dead, for they remain bound up with the earthly sphere. And once the human soul is no longer separated from its surroundings by a body that would prevent it from acting in a destructive way, this human soul becomes a focus of destruction within the earthly sphere.

It has to be said that this is quite a normal situation. Under today's conditions, souls who enter the spiritual world after death, having wanted to know absolutely nothing about spiritual concepts and feelings, become focuses of destruction because they are detained in the earthly sphere. Only those souls who have already here been filled with a degree of connection with the spiritual world pass through the gate of death in such a way that they are taken up into the spiritual world in the right way and removed from the earthly sphere; they can spin the threads in the right way that link them with those who have remained behind, threads which are continually spun. We must not forget that the spiritual threads linking the dead souls with those of us here who have been connected with them are not sundered by death; they remain and even become much more intimate after death than they were here. What I have been describing must be accepted as a serious and important truth.

Once again the fact that this is how things are at the present time is something known not only to me but to others as well. There are some who make use of the truth in a really nasty way. Today there are those who have been duped into believing that nothing exists except the material life. But there are also initiates who are materialists and who make sure that brotherhoods spread materialistic teachings. Do not believe that these initiates take the ridiculous view that there is no spirit, or that human beings do not have souls that can be independent of the body and live without it. You may be sure that anyone properly initiated into the spiritual world would not subscribe to the absurd notion of believing only in matter. But there are many who are in one way or another interested in spreading materialism and who make all kinds of arrangements to ensure that a great part of humanity believes only in materialism and is entirely under the influence of materialism. There are brotherhoods headed by initiates who are interested in cultivating and spreading materialism. These materialists are very well served by all the talk about materialism having already been overcome. Aims can be pursued by opposing words; indeed, the way of going about things is often quite complicated.

So what do those initiates want who know very well that the human soul is a purely spiritual being which is entirely independent of the body, and who nevertheless want to cultivate people's materialistic outlook? These initiates want to ensure that as many souls as possible only take in materialistic thoughts here between birth and death. By this means, such souls are prepared in a way that forces them to remain within the earth's sphere. They are held within the sphere of the earth. Then consider that brotherhoods are set up who know all about this. These brotherhoods prepare certain human souls in a way that makes them remain in the material realm after death. If these brotherhoods then also bring it about that these souls come within their sphere of influence after death — which may well lie within their villainous power — then that brotherhood gains a huge amount of power. These materialists are not materialists because they do not believe in the spirit; these materialistic initiates are not so stupid. They know very well what are the implications of the spirit. But they cause the souls to remain within matter even after death in order to make use of them for their own purposes. They create a clientele of dead souls that remain within the sphere of the earth. These dead souls possess forces that can be guided in various ways which make it possible to gain quite specific powers over those who are not party to such things.

This is quite simply something that certain brotherhoods set in train. And this is seen clearly only by those who are not prepared to believe in anything that is obscure or nebulous, and who do not allow themselves to be persuaded either that such brotherhoods do not exist or that what they do is harmless. These things are not at all harmless; they are very harmful, for the intention is to make human beings go further and further into materialism. What these initiates want is for these human beings to believe that although spiritual forces do exist they are nothing but forces of nature.

Let me now characterize the ideal held by such brotherhoods. You will have to make some effort to understand the matter. Think of an innocuous human world which has been led astray a little by the prevailing materialistic concepts of today and which has deviated somewhat from ancient, well-tried religious ideas. Think of an innocuous humanity of this kind. Perhaps it can be depicted graphically [*the speaker draws*]. Here is the realm of that innocuous humanity [*larger circle, pale*]. As I have said, this humanity is not only not quite clear regarding the spiritual world; it has also been led astray by materialism and does not quite know how to behave as regards the spiritual world. In

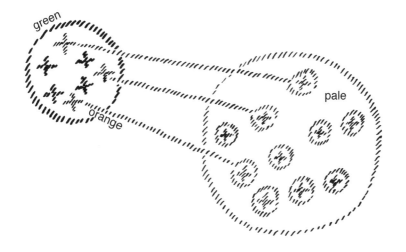

particular this humanity does not quite know what to do about those who have passed through the gate of death.

So now let us assume that here is the realm of one of those brotherhoods [*small circle, green*]. This brotherhood is spreading the doctrine of materialism and ensuring that these human beings most probably think in a purely materialistic way. By this means the brotherhood succeeds in generating souls for itself that remain in the earthly sphere after death. They become the spiritual clientele of this lodge [*orange*]. In other words, by this means dead souls have been created who do not go out of the earthly sphere but remain with the earth. By making the right arrangements they can be held within the lodge. So in this way lodges have been created which contain the living but also the dead, the dead who have become related to the earthly forces.

Matters are then directed by these people here who hold sessions or by means of arranging meetings like the spiritualist seances of the second half of the nineteenth century about which I have frequently spoken.[9] It can then happen — and please take note of this — that what goes on here in the sessions is directed by the lodge with the help of the dead. But it is the intention of the masters in those lodges that the people must not know that they are dealing with the dead, for they are meant to believe that what they are dealing with are simply higher forces of nature. The intention is to show people that these are higher forces of nature, psychism and so on, merely higher forces of nature. The concept of the soul as such is taken away and the people are told: 'Just as there is electricity, and magnetism, so are there similar higher forces.' Those who lead the lodge hide the fact that these things are coming from souls. So those other, innocuous souls gradually become dependent, psychologically dependent, on the lodge without knowing what they are dependent on or where that which is directing them is coming from.

The only defence against these things is knowing about them. If you know about them you are protected. If you know about them in that you really regard them as true, that you really believe them to be like this, then you are protected. But you must not be idle about acquiring real knowledge about these things. For the present, however, it can still be said that it is not yet absolutely too late regarding this. These things can only be clarified gradually and I can only slowly gather together the various elements by which you can be given full clarity. But meanwhile I have often told you that during the second half of the nineteenth century many brotherhoods of the West introduced spiritualism as an experiment.[10] They wanted to test whether they had already reached the stage they intended with regard to humanity. It was an experiment to test how far they had progressed with humanity. What they intended —

and indeed expected — was that during spiritualist seances people should say: 'Higher forces of nature do indeed exist.' But the brothers of the left-hand path were then disappointed when most people said instead: 'The spirits of the dead appear during the seances.' This was a bitter disappointment for the initiates, for it was exactly what they did not want. Belief in the dead was the very thing which they wanted to take away from human beings. People were to be deprived not of the workings of the dead, not of the way the forces of the dead worked, but of the thought, that very significant thought, that these things do come from the dead.

As you can see, this is a higher form of materialism, a materialism that not only denies the existence of the spirit but that wants to imprison the spirit in matter. Materialism still manifests in ways that make it possible to deny its existence. People can say that materialism has gone and that what we are talking about is spirit. But they all speak about the spirit in a vague way. Making all nature into spirit in a way that leads to psychism as the end result is a very good way of being a materialist. But what really matters is the ability to see into the concrete spiritual world, into concrete spirituality.

This, then, is the beginning of something that will become more and more intensive over the coming five centuries. The evil brotherhoods have now restricted themselves to this, but they will surely continue in their efforts if we do not put a stop to their handiwork; and the only way to put a stop to it is to overcome our idleness with regard to the world view of spiritual science.

In some ways they rather gave the game away in the spiritualist seances. Instead of covering their tracks they laid bare their tracks through those spiritualist seances which showed that their machinations were not yet particularly successful. So then, from the 1890s onwards, those very brotherhoods set about discrediting spiritualism for the time being. In short, you can see that by these means very, very incisive interventions are being made by using the spiritual world. They aim to increase their power and utilize certain conditions of evolution that must obtain during the course of human progress.

There is something that is working to counteract the materialization of human souls, the imprisonment of human souls in the sphere of earthliness — where the lodges also have their existence. If the souls are to go about their ghostly work in the lodges they have to be imprisoned in the earthly sphere. But this endeavour, this impulse to work through these souls in the earthly sphere is being counteracted by the remarkable impulse of the Mystery of Golgotha. This impulse of the Mystery of Golgotha provides the universal healing to counteract the materialization of the soul. The pathway of Christ exists entirely outside the will and intentions of human beings. No human being of whatever persuasion, not even any initiate, can influence Christ in doing what leads to his appearance during the course of the twentieth century about which I have often spoken to you and which you will also find hinted at in the Mystery Plays. This depends solely on Christ himself. Christ will be present as an etheric being in the sphere of earth. But as to how human beings behave towards him, that will be up to them. No one, not even the mightiest initiate, can have any influence on Christ's appearance as such. Please do remember this. But it is possible to arrange affairs in ways that could lead to this Christ Event being received either in one way or in another way, and being effective either in one way or in another way.

The brotherhoods I have just mentioned, the ones who want to imprison human souls in the material sphere, are aiming to make Christ's appearance pass by unnoticed in the twentieth century; their aim is to prevent people from noticing his arrival as an etheric individuality. This endeavour is developing under the influence of a specific idea, or rather a specific impulse of will. On behalf of an entirely different being the brotherhoods want to seize and conquer the sphere of influence that is supposed to come about through Christ in the twentieth century and beyond. (We shall refer to this in more detail later.) There are western brotherhoods who are striving to deprive Christ of his impulse and put in its place a different individuality, one who has never even been on earth in the flesh—a purely etheric individuality, albeit a strictly ahrimanic one.

All the measures I have been speaking about—to do with the dead and so on—ultimately all of these serve the aims of distracting human beings from Christ, who passed through the Mystery of Golgotha, and of wangling affairs in ways that will give another individuality dominance over the earth. This battle is entirely real and not at all a matter of abstractions. It is a battle that aims to put another being in the place belonging to the Christ Being for the remainder of the fifth post-Atlantean age, and also for the sixth and the seventh. One of the tasks of a healthy and honest spiritual development will be to exterminate and remove those endeavours, which are eminently anti-Christian.

Clear insight alone, however, will be able to achieve this. For the brotherhoods will give the name of 'Christ', the actual name of 'Christ', to that other being whom they want to make into the ruler. It will therefore be crucial to learn to distinguish between the true Christ, who this time will also be an individuality not incarnated in the flesh, and that other being who differs from the true Christ in that he has never been incarnated throughout earthly evolution but whom those brotherhoods now want to install in the place of Christ who, they intend, shall pass by unnoticed.

So here we have the part of the battle that relates to falsifying the Christ-appearance of the twentieth century. Those who look only at the surface of life, especially all those superficial discussions about Christ and the Jesus question and so on, they cannot see into the depths. A great deal of fog and hot air is produced in order to distract people from the profounder matters that are really at issue. When theologians have discussions about Christ there is always, from somewhere or other, some spiritual influence, so that these people are really helping to promote aims and purposes that are quite different from what they consciously believe.

This is what is so dangerous about the concept of the unconscious. Whereas the evil brotherhoods follow their aims very consciously, these things that they follow consciously become what is unconscious in those who get involved in all kinds of superficial discussions. To talk of the unconscious is to bypass the core of the matter, for this so-called unconscious is simply what lies beyond the threshold of ordinary consciousness, and this is the sphere where those who are in the know can develop such things. So you see, this is really one side of the matter which confronts a number of brotherhoods who want to replace the working of Christ by the working of another individuality through arranging everything in favour of achieving this.

On the other hand there are eastern brotherhoods, especially Indian ones, who also want to interfere in human evolution in a manner no less significant. These Indian brotherhoods are pursuing a different aim. They have never

developed esoteric practices by which they can imprison
the dead in their realm, in the realm of their lodges. Such
things are very far from what they want. But they also do
not want the impulse of the Mystery of Golgotha to play its
part in the evolution of humanity. This is not because they
do not have the dead at their disposal in the way I have
described in connection with the western brotherhoods.
They do not want to fight against Christ—who will enter
into human evolution as an etheric invaluality during the
course of the twentieth century—by setting up another
individuality in his place; to do this they would need the
dead, whom they do not have. What they want to do is
deflect interest away from Christ. These eastern brotherhoods, especially the Indian ones, do not want Christianity
to become a force to be reckoned with. They do not want
any interest in the real Christ to develop, the real Christ
who endured the Mystery of Golgotha and who was on the
earth for three years in a single incarnation and who cannot
again incarnate on the earth. They do not want to make use
of the dead in their lodges, yet they do also want something
different from what they are as living human beings. In
these Indian, eastern lodges use is made of beings that are
different from the dead of the western lodges.

When a human being dies the etheric body is left behind
which very soon separates off after death, as you know.
Under normal circumstances this etheric body is absorbed
by the cosmos, and I have shown you in various ways that
this process of absorption is complicated.[11] Before the
Mystery of Golgotha, however, and also after the Mystery
of Golgotha, especially in eastern regions, something quite
specific was possible. When a human being relinquishes his
ether body after death, certain specific beings can enter into
it. With these ether bodies relinquished by human beings

they become etheric beings. So it can happen in eastern regions that not dead human beings but all kinds of demonic spirits are caused to dress up in abandoned human ether bodies. And these demonic spirits clothed in human ether bodies are then received by the eastern lodges. The western lodges have the dead who are imprisoned in matter; the eastern lodges of the left-hand path have demonic spirits, that is, spirits who do not belong to earthly evolution but who creep into earthly evolution by putting on ether bodies laid aside by human beings.

Exoterically this is done by transforming this fact into worship. You know that certain brotherhoods practise the art of calling forth illusions because when people are unaware of the degree to which illusion is present in reality they are very easily duped by artificially produced illusions. So to achieve what is required it is disguised as worship. Imagine a clan of people who belong together. First of all, as an 'evil' brother, one has to prepare for the ether body of an ancestor to be occupied by a demonic being. Then one says to the members of the clan that they must worship that ancestor. The ancestor is simply the one who has laid aside his ether body into which demons have been moved by the machinations of the lodge. In other words, one introduces ancestor worship. But the ancestors who are worshipped are merely demonic beings of some kind in the ether body of the real ancestor.

The way in which eastern people look at the world can be turned aside from the Mystery of Golgotha by working in the way those eastern lodges work. The consequence for the eastern people is then, and perhaps for everyone (for this is, after all, the aim), that the goal is achieved whereby Christ, who is to move above the earth as an individuality, remains unnoticed. Those who do this do not want to substitute another being for Christ, they simply want the appearance of Christ Jesus to pass unnoticed.

In this way battle is being waged from two directions against the etheric appearance of the Christ-impulse during the course of the twentieth century. This is what is really going on around humanity. And whatever happens individually is really always only a consequence of the overall impulses in human evolution. This is why it is so sad when efforts keep being made to persuade people that when the unconscious, the so-called unconscious, works in them it is the result of repressed love or something similar, whereas in fact the impulse of very conscious spirituality is being brought in to move about amongst humanity from all sides which, though, remains relatively unconscious if one does not make efforts in one's consciousness to be aware of it.

You must add various other facts to all this. People who have ever been well disposed towards human evolution have always reckoned with matters such as the ones we have just been describing. For their part they have done what was right—and in fact one cannot and may not do much more.

One very good place where spiritual life was cultivated during the early centuries of Christianity was Ireland, the island of Ireland. This island was thoroughly protected, more protected than anywhere else on earth, against all kinds of illusons. That is also the reason why so many who disseminated Christianity in those early Christian centuries set out from Ireland. Those spreaders of Christianity all had to bear in mind that they were working amongst naïve human beings, for the European humanity amongst whom they were working was naïve, and allowances had to be made for their naïvety. At the same time they had to know about and understand the great impulses of humanity. Irish initiates, chiefly, were at work during the fourth and fifth centuries in Central Europe. That is where they began, and they worked to prepare for what must happen in the future. The initiation knowledge that influenced them was that in the fifteenth century—you know, 1413—the fifth post-Atlantean age would arrive. This is what influenced them, so they knew that they were having to prepare an entirely new age, and for this new age humanity had to be protected so that it would remain naïve.

What was done in those days to ensure that Europe's humanity would be fenced round in order to prevent certain harmful influences from entering? From a knowledgeable and honest quarter guidance for evolution came that gradually caused the maritime traffic going from the northern countries to America in those olden times to cease.[12] So whereas in those olden times ships sailed to America especially from Norway for certain purposes, it was gradually brought about that America was entirely forgotten by the population of Europe and the connection with America disappeared. In the fifteenth century the people of Europe knew nothing about America. Because European humanity had to be protected against influences from America, matters were directed, especially from Rome, in ways that caused the links with America to be lost. Some who were very influential in protecting European humanity against influences from America were those very monks who, as Irish initiates, set out from Ireland to bring Christianity to Europe.

In those older times certain quite specific influences were brought back from America. But at the time when the fifth post-Atlantean epoch was beginning it was important that the European population remained uninfluenced by America, knew nothing about it and lived in the belief that no such land existed. It was rediscovered once the fifth post-Atlantean age had begun, as historians tell us. One of the truths that you are surely familiar with is that the history we learn in school is frequently a legend. That America was discovered for the first time in 1492 is a legend, for in fact that is when it was rediscovered. For a time it had remained as thoroughly hidden as was necessary. We ought to know what the real situation was and what the genuine history is, namely, that for a period Europe was fenced round and carefully protected against certain influences that had to be prevented from entering there.

Such things show how meaningful it is to regard the so-called unconscious not as something that is unconscious but as something that takes place very consciously beyond the threshold of everyday human consciousness. And it is important today that humanity should hear about certain secrets. That is why I have done as much as is possible at the moment to speak quite openly. As you know, in the lectures in Zurich I even went so far as to explain to people about the degree to which they do not know historical life in their ordinary consciousness but that in reality they dream it.[13] I said that in reality the content of history is dreamt by people and that their ideas about it will only become healthy once they realize that the content of history is dreamt.

It is through things like this that consciousness can gradually be awakened. The way facts manifest shows the truth in this, only one must not overlook it. People are blind and asleep in the way they make their way through facts; they are also blind and asleep in making their way through tragic catastrophes like those of today. Today I wanted to draw your attention to these matters concerning history, and tomorrow I shall speak in more detail.

I want to make one more point in connection with all this.

Firstly, from all that has been said you have seen what a tremendous difference there is in the evolution of humanity between the West and the East. Secondly, please take also the following into consideration.

Psychoanalysts speak of the subconscious, of the sub-conscious life of the soul and so on. But such an inde-terminate concept is not the point. The point is the question: What is there beyond the threshold of consciousness? What exists there? There is certainly a great deal down there beneath the threshold of consciousness. But in itself what is down there is very conscious. However, one must become aware of what it is, that conscious spirituality beyond the threshold of consciousness. One must speak of conscious spirituality beyond the threshold of consciousness, not of unconscious spirituality. One must realize that human beings have a great deal about which they know nothing in their ordinary consciousness. In fact, it would be most awkward if they had to be aware in their ordinary con-sciousness of all that goes on inside them. Think of how they would cope with eating and drinking if they had to know exactly what takes place physiologically and biolo-gically when food is eaten, and so on! All this takes place in the unconscious, and in all of it, even these purely physio-logical processes, spiritual forces are at work. But human beings cannot put off eating and drinking until they have learnt about all that goes on inside them. Many other things go on inside them as well. In fact, the greater part, indeed the greatest part of their being is unconscious, or rather subconscious.

The remarkable thing is that in every instance another being takes possession of this subconscious that we carry with us. We are therefore not only a combination of body, soul and spirit in which we carry about within our body the soul which is independent of us, for shortly before we are born another being takes possession of the subconscious parts of our being. This subconscious being accompanies us for the whole length of the journey between birth and death. It enters shortly before we are born and then remains with us.

To describe this being that fills the parts of us that do not enter into ordinary consciousness, we can say that it is a very intelligent being, one in which the will resembles the forces of nature. It is a being that is very intelligent and which is endowed with a will that is very like the forces of nature, much more so than is the human will. It has one characteristic which must be emphasized, and that is that it would suffer great danger if, under present conditions, it were to enter into death together with the human being. Under present conditions this being cannot share in death, so it absconds shortly before death because it has to save itself. Nevertheless, its endeavour is to arrange human life in such a way that it becomes able to win power over death.

For human evolution it would be terrible if this being that takes possession of the human being were also able to win power over death, if it were able to die with the human being and in this way enter into those worlds which we enter after death. It always has to take leave of us before we step into the spiritual world after death. But it can find this quite a difficult thing to do and all kinds of complications can ensue. The fact of the matter is that this being, which holds sway entirely in the subconscious, is very, very dependent on the earth as a whole organism.

The earth is not at all the kind of being presented to us by geologists, mineralogists or palaeontologists, for it is in fact a being full of life. All we see of it is its skeleton, for geologists, mineralogists and palaeontologists present us solely with the mineral part, the bony structure. If that is the only aspect of the earth you know about, then you know more or less as much as you would know about the present distinguished company if you came in here with a special kind of sight that allowed you to see only the bones, the skeletal system. Imagine coming in through the door and seeing rows of skeletons sitting on the seats. Of course I don't mean to suggest that there is nothing more to you than bones, but if a person could see only bones it would be as though he were seeing through some kind of X-ray machine. This is all that geologists see of the earth, nothing more than the skeleton.

The earth, however, has more than a skeleton, for it is a living organism. And from its centre it sends out specific forces to every location, every territory on its surface.

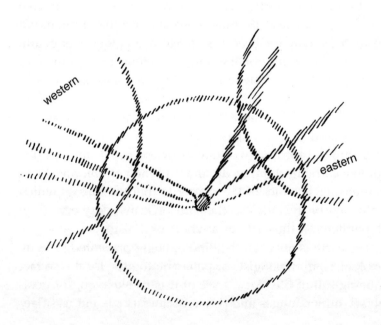

Imagine the surface of the earth with an eastern region here and a western one there, to mention only the large-scale situation. The forces sent up out of the earth come from the earth's life organism. When a person lives on the earth at one location or another it is not—or only indirectly—his soul, his immortal soul that comes into contact with these forces of the earth. The human being's immortal soul is relatively very independent of earthly conditions; it is only made dependent on these conditions artificially, as I showed you today. But through that other being which takes possession of the human being before birth and has to depart before death, via a detour through that other being the various forces work especially strongly through racial types and geographical variations. So the geographical and other differences work especially on the double which every human being carries.

This is exceedingly significant. Tomorrow we shall see how different effects impinge on this double at different locations on the earth, and what the consequences are. As I told you, it will be necessary for you to make a close connection between what I am telling you today and what I shall say tomorrow since the one will be barely comprehensible without the other. We must endeavour to understand concepts that take seriously the whole of reality, that reality in which the whole being of the human soul lives. This reality, however, metamorphoses in various ways, and these ways depend greatly on the individual human being. One significant metamorphosis is how, depending on whether they absorb materialistic or spiritual concepts between birth and death, human souls correspondingly tie themselves to the earth or can enter into the right spheres. Amongst ourselves we must always have clear concepts about these things; then we shall also gain the right relationship with the world at large, in fact we must find such a relationship more and more. For us it is not merely a matter of some abstract spiritual movement. Our concern is with a spiritual movement that is entirely concrete and that reckons with the spiritual life of a whole accumulation of individuals.

For me it is very satisfying that talks of this kind are especially significant for those amongst us who no longer belong to the physical plane but who have passed through the gate of death although they remain our faithful co-members. It is satisfying that such talks are cultivated as a reality that unites us ever more deeply with those of our friends who have departed. I say this because we should today remember with special love the departure of Fraülein Stinde who was so intimately bound up with our building here, whose impulses were so intimately linked with the impulses of our building, and the anniversary of whose death fell yesterday.[14]

Dornach, 19 November 1917

6. Individual Spirit Beings and the Constant Foundation of the Universe, II

With regard to our present considerations, which I have linked to a description of an endeavour to find knowledge by inadequate means and which have now led us to a wider historical perspective, let me begin both in this connection and in connection with what I said last time I spoke here — with the same purpose and out of the same impulse — by begging you to realize that I am talking about actual events, not some theory, not some system of ideas, but facts. This is the point we must be clear about because otherwise it will be difficult to understand these things. Rather than propounding historical laws or ideas I am telling you facts, facts that are connected with the intentions not only of certain individuals who are joined together in brotherhoods but also of other beings who influence such brotherhoods and whose influence is also sought by those brotherhoods, beings who are not incarnated in the flesh like human beings but ones who have their body in the spiritual world.

It is especially necessary to take account of this in the case of a fact such as the one I told you about yesterday. As I explained last year,[1] these brotherhoods belong to different factions. I showed you last year that amongst these brotherhoods there is one faction that is in favour of absolute secrecy about certain higher truths. Then, besides other shades of opinion, there are, especially since the middle of the nineteenth century, members of brotherhoods who are in favour of revealing certain truths to humanity carefully and with the necessary objectivity, but only those truths which it is immediately necessary to reveal. There are other nuances in addition to these two main factions. So you can see that the intentions, the impulses inserted by those brotherhoods into the evolution of humanity are likely to be a matter of compromise quite frequently.

Those brotherhoods who know about the spiritual impulses at work in human evolution saw the approach of that important event of the early 1840s, the battle between certain spirits and some other higher spirits which ended in 1879 when some spirits of an angel nature, spirits of darkness, fell victim to the event that is symbolized as the victory of Michael over the dragon. On seeing this, those brotherhoods had to decide how to react to it and had to ask themselves: What is to be done about it?

Some members of the brotherhoods who wanted to do what was right for that time were to some degree motivated by the best intentions. But they were influenced by the erroneous impression that it was necessary to take account of the materialism of that time. As people anyway wanted to know about things in a physical way, those members of the brotherhoods were intent on teaching them something about the spiritual world by materialistic means in a physical way. So it was out of good intentions that spiritualism was launched in the world during the 1840s.

That battle took place, as I have pointed out, at a time when the attitude on earth was supposed to be a mainly critical one, an understanding directed solely towards the external world. It was necessary, then, that people had to be given at least an inkling, a sense for the fact that there was a spiritual world all around them. And so, as happens with compromises, this compromise came about. Those members of such brotherhoods who were entirely against certain spiritual truths being made known to humanity found themselves overruled and had to give in and agree to the matter. It was not their original intention to put about in the world things that were connected with spiritualism. But where there are corporate bodies, and where there is the will of corporate bodies, compromise ensues. And just as things are in external life, so are they in corporations: When a corporate body makes a decision, those who for their own reasons have worked towards this decision expect something from it; but those who were originally against it also have expectations once the decision has been made.

Well-meaning spiritual members of the brotherhoods held the erroneous view that by using mediums they could convince people of the existence of a spiritual world all around them; and they thought that on the basis of that conviction it would then be possible to teach them about higher truths as well. This would indeed have been possible if the expectations of those well-meaning members of the brotherhoods had been realized, namely, if what the mediums revealed had been interpreted as a sign that this was connected with a surrounding spiritual world. But something quite different happened, as I showed you yesterday. People who participated in these things interpreted what came through the mediums as coming from the dead.

So what came about through spiritualism actually turned out to be disappointing for everyone. Those who had allowed themselves to be persuaded were naturally exceedingly disconcerted by the fact that one could talk of the spirits of the dead manifesting in the seances—especially as this was true in some cases. And the well-meaning progressive initiates had not expected any mention to be made of the dead, for they had thought people would talk of a general, elementary world; so they, too, were disappointed. Those who have been initiated in some way are primarily the ones who take note of such things.

Apart from the already mentioned members of brotherhoods there are also those who are members of other, or even the same, brotherhoods in which minorities, or even majorities, sometimes form. These other initiates must also be taken into account, and they are those within the brotherhoods who are termed 'brothers of the left-hand path', namely, those who make use above all of every kind of impulse involving matters of power that can be brought into human evolution.[2]

These brothers of the left-hand path in their turn also had all kinds of expectations about what came to light through spiritualism. I pointed out yesterday that brothers of the left-hand path were, in particular, those who made arrangements in connection with the souls of dead human beings. They were especially interested in what might come out of spiritualist seances. Gradually they took charge of this whole field of activity. The well-meaning initiates gradually lost all interest in spiritualism and indeed felt ashamed in some ways because those who from the beginning had not wanted spiritualism told them that they ought to have known from the start that nothing could come of it. This is how spiritualism then came to be taken over by, let us say, the power zone of the brothers of the left-hand path.

Yesterday I mentioned those brothers of the left-hand path who were most of all disappointed when they saw that once spiritualism had been launched it might reveal the very thing set in train by them which they least of all wanted to have exposed. Those spiritualist seances where the participants believed they were being influenced by the dead might provide the very venue where messages from the dead could reveal what certain brothers of the left-hand path did with the souls of those who have died. Perhaps those very souls who had been misused by the brothers of the left-hand path would be the ones to manifest during the spiritualist seances.

You must please remember that I am not speaking about theories but about facts derived from individual people. And if those individuals are gathered together in brotherhoods, one of them might expect one thing from a fact and another something else from the same fact. When one is speaking about real facts of the spiritual world it is not possible to seek there anything that is not the result of individual impulses. In ordinary life, too, what one person does can contradict what another does. Theoretically the law of contradictions cannot be gainsaid. And where facts are concerned it happens frequently that facts in the spiritual world, too, are just as likely to be in disharmony as actions of human beings here on the physical plane. You must please always take this into account. In these matters one cannot speak of realities if one does not speak of individual facts. So one must distinguish between the separate streams; one must peel them apart.

This is connected with something very important which we must be especially aware of if we want to arrive at a relatively satisfying view of the world. What I am going to say now is a matter of principle and very important even though it is somewhat abstract. It is a fact to which we must for once pay attention.

When working towards forming our view of the world we strive, quite justifiably, to make sure that the different parts of our world view harmonize with one another. We do this out of a degree of habit that could not be more justifiable for it is bound up with all that has been humanity's most beloved treasure of soul and spirit for many centuries: monotheism. We want whatever we experience in the world to be traceable to a unifying foundation. This is entirely justifiable, but not from the angle people usually assume, with justification, but from an entirely different angle about which we shall speak next time. Today I only want to put before your souls what is principally important.

Those whose approach to the world assumes that everything must be explicable without contradiction owing to having been derived from a unifying foundation of the universe, those who have this assumption are in for many disappointments especially if they make their approach to the world and its experiences with an open mind. This is so traditionally ingrained that we treat everything we see in the world in accordance with the pastoral view: everything is derived from a unifying, divine, original foundation; everything stems from God so there must be a uniform explanation for everything.

But this is not true. It is not so that all the experiences which surround us in the world stem from a unifying foundation, for in fact everything stems from spiritual individualities who differ from one another. Various individualities join together to bring about the experiences that surround us in the world. Initially, this is how things are. Next time we shall speak about other aspects, which make monotheism justifiable, but in the first instance this is how things are. As soon as we step across the threshold of the spiritual world we must imagine individualities who are rather independent, in fact very independent, of one another. And if this is so, then we cannot expect everything that happens to be explicable on the basis of a single unifying principle.

Let us draw an experience, let's say the experiences from 1913 to 1918. (Of course there are experiences before and after as well.)

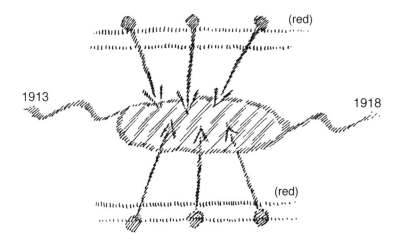

Historians will always endeavour to assume that there is a unifying principle manifesting in this developmental path. But there is not. Once we step across the threshold to the spiritual world, it does not matter whether upwards or downwards [*red*], we find at work in these events various individualities who are relatively independent of one another [*arrows*]. If you do not take this into account, if you assume that a unifying world foundation underlies everything, you will never reach an understanding of the events. You will only understand them properly if you take account of the fact that very varied individualities work either against or with one another in what might be termed the groundswell of events.

All this is linked to the profoundest mysteries of human evolution; but the monotheistic feeling has concealed this fact for centuries, even millennia. It must, though, be taken into account. So if we want to make progress in matters of a world view today, we must above all not mistake logic for abstract absence of contradiction. There can be no abstract absence of contradiction in a world where individualities who are independent from one another work together. So whenever the aim is to achieve an abstract lack of contradiction, this will lead to an impoverishment of concepts; concepts will no longer be able to encompass the fullness of reality. Concepts can only encompass the fullness of reality if they are able to embrace that world of contradictions which is, in fact, reality.

The sphere of nature we see before us comes into being in a remarkable way. Various individualities work together to create nature, everything we call nature and summarize on the one hand as natural science and on the other as nature worship, nature aesthetics and so on. But in the present cycle of human evolution a wise guidance has seen to it that a very beneficial arrangement has been made for us. This enables us to conceive of nature by means of concepts relating to a unifying regulation because through our senses we receive only those experiences of it that depend on such a unifying regulation. Behind the tapestry of nature, however, there lies something else which receives its direction from quite another quarter. This, though, is excluded from our observation of nature.

So what we call nature is indeed a unified system because everything else has been screened out. It is as though we perceive nature through the filter of our senses. Everything that is contradictory is filtered out and the nature we have before us is thus a unified system. Once we cross the threshold, however, and include reality in our explanation of nature — the elemental beings, influences of human souls that can be directed towards nature — then we can no longer talk of nature as being a unified system. For then we also have to include the workings of individualities who either obstruct one another or support and strengthen one another.

In the elemental world there are spirits of earth, gnome-like beings; spirits of water, undine-like beings; spirits of air, sylph-like beings; and spirits of fire, salamander-like beings. They are all present there, but they do not carry on a unified regimen. These various realms — the gnomes, undines, sylphs and salamanders — are independent of one another in some ways; they work not only in rank and file as part of a single system, but they also oppose one another. Their intentions are not linked from the beginning, so what comes about arises from the various ways in which their intentions mutually affect one another. If we know the intentions, we can see in what appears before us, for example: Here are fire spirits and undines working together. But we must never believe that there is a single being behind them giving them commands, for this is not the case.

It is an attitude much held these days. Philosophers like Wundt[3] (of whom Fritz Mauthner[4] said, not without reason, that he was an authority by the grace of his publisher, for indeed before the war he was regarded as an authority by almost the entire world) assume that the life of ideas, of feelings and of will — everything living in the human soul — all belong in a single unit. They say: The soul is a unit, so all these must have a single system in common. But this is not true. Those powerful and significant discrepancies found in human life especially by analytical psychology would not occur if, beyond the threshold, our life of ideas did not reach back into regions where it is influenced by individualities different from those influencing our feeling life and different again from those of our life of will.

It's quite extraordinary! Look, here is the human soul [*drawing, oval*], and within the human soul are the life of ideas, the life of feeling and the life of will [*three circles*]. Someone like Wundt who likes systems cannot imagine this to be anything but one single system.

Life of ideas

Life of feeling

Life of will

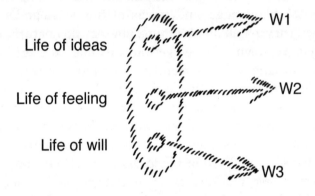

Yet the life of ideas leads to one world (W1), the life of feeling to another world (W2), and the life of will to another world again (W3). That is the very function of the human soul, to create a unit for something that is threefold in the pre-human world as matters stand at present.

Account has to be taken of all these things when one considers the impulses that are to be incorporated into human evolution.

I have said during these lectures that every period of the post-Atlantean age has its own specific task,[5] and I have given a general description of the task of the fifth post-Atlantean period by saying that it will be up to humanity during this period to come to grips with evil as an impulse in world evolution. We have talked variously about what this means. It is essential that the forces which manifest as evil if they appear at the wrong place must be taken in hand by human endeavour in the fifth post-Atlantean period in such a way that humanity can achieve something with these forces of evil that will be beneficial for the future of the whole of world evolution. Because of this the task of this fifth post-Atlantean period is an especially difficult one.

You see, a great many temptations will be visited on humanity as time goes on. When little by little the powers of evil make their appearance, human beings may naturally be much more inclined to give in to this evil in every field instead of taking up the fight to bring what seems evil to them into the service of world evolution in the sense of what is good. Yet this is what must come about: to a certain degree evil must be placed at the service of world evolution in the good sense. Failing this it will be impossible to enter into the sixth post-Atlantean period, which will have an entirely different task. Although human beings will still be linked with the earth, the task will be to enable them to look continuously into the spiritual world and live in spiritual impulses. Connected with the task of the fifth post-Atlantean period concerning evil there is the possibility that a certain kind of personal darkening for human beings could arise.

As we know, since 1879 there have been within the human kingdom spirits of darkness who are the next closest to humanity and belong to the kingdom of the Angeloi. They are here because they have been turned out of the spiritual world, so now they live in and through human impulses. The fact that there are beings invisibly amongst us who are so closely related to human beings, and that human beings are prevented by the way forces of evil play into their lives from recognizing the spirit with their reason — which is the task of the fifth post-Atlantean period related to this — means that in this fifth post-Atlantean period there will be many opportunities for people to succumb to obscure errors and suchlike. During this fifth post-Atlantean period we must make the effort to comprehend the spiritual through our reason. The spirit will be revealed, that is certain. Because the spirits of darkness were overcome in 1879, more and more spiritual wisdom will be able to flow down from the spiritual worlds, for those spirits would only have been able to prevent this if they had remained up above in the realms of spirit. They can no longer prevent spiritual wisdom from flowing down, but what they can do is create confusion and bring obscurity to human souls. The opportunities that are being taken to create this obscurity have already been described to some extent.[6] We have already talked about the kind of arrangements that are being made to prevent human beings from receiving the life of the spirit.

All this does not, of course, give cause for lamentation and suchlike but provides a strengthening of the power and energy of the human soul in its leaning towards the spirit. If what can be achieved is achieved by human beings during this fifth post-Atlantean period through incorporating the forces of evil in the good sense, then at the same time something else, something tremendous, will also be achieved: the fifth post-Atlantean period will then know something grander for the evolution of humanity than has ever been known by any other, any earlier period of earth evolution. For example, Christ appeared to the fourth post-Atlantean period through the Mystery of Golgotha; but only now can the fifth post-Atlantean period absorb him by human reason. Human beings in the fourth post-Atlantean period were able to comprehend that in the Christ-impulse they had something that would lead them, as souls, beyond death; that has been made sufficiently clear by Pauline Christianity. But something even more significant will occur for the development of the fifth post-Atlantean period when human souls recognize that in Christ they have the helper they need to transform the forces of evil into good.

There is one thing connected with this feature of the fifth post-Atlantean period, one thing which one should inscribe anew into one's soul every day, one thing which one should not forget even though human beings are particularly prone to forget this particular thing. This is that in this fifth post-Atlantean period the human being must be a warrior for the spirit; human beings must experience how their forces ebb away if they do not continuously hold them in check for the purpose of winning through to the spiritual world. In this fifth post-Atlantean period human beings stand on their freedom to the highest degree! This is something they have to go through with. The idea of human freedom is the yardstick against which must be measured everything that human beings meet with during this fifth post-Atlantean period. For were their forces to weaken, this could cause everything to turn out for the worst. In this fifth post-Atlantean period human beings are not in the situation of being led like children. If there are certain brotherhoods whose ideal it is to lead human beings like children, as they were led in the third post-Atlantean period, and in the fourth, then these brotherhoods are not doing what is right; they are not doing what actually ought to be done for the evolution of humanity.

Anyone who speaks about the spiritual world must do so in a way that leaves people free to accept or reject what he is saying. Someone speaking about the spiritual world in this fifth post-Atlantean period must constantly remind himself of this. Because of this certain things can only be said in this fifth post-Atlantean period, and the actual saying of these things is now just as important as anything else was in other periods. I will give you an example of what I mean.

In our time, the most important thing is to bring forward truths—put plainly, to give lectures about truths. What people then do about this is up to their freedom. One should go no further than to lecture on, to communicate truths. Whatever consequences there are should follow as a free decision, just as consequences follow when decisions are made out of the impulses one has on the physical plane. It is exactly the same in the case of things that can only be guided from the spiritual world itself.

It will be easier to understand this if we go into some detail. Even as late as the fourth post-Atlantean period other things besides the word, besides mere information, came into consideration. What were these? Let us take a specific example. The island of Ireland, as we call it today, has some quite special features. Certain characteristics make this island of Ireland different from any other place on earth. Every region of the earth differs from the others in certain respects, so as such this is nothing out of the ordinary. Today, though, I want to stress the relatively marked difference that exists between Ireland and other parts of the earth. As you know from my book *An Outline of Esoteric Science*,[7] by looking at the facts that can be gleaned from the spiritual world we can go back in time and note certain influences and events in the evolution of the earth. You know from *An Outline* how things were in what we call the age of Lemuria, you know what went on in that age and how various aspects developed.

Well, yesterday I drew your attention to the necessity of

viewing the earth as an organism and how in different regions it sends out different streams that influence the inhabitants. These streams of influence have a particular effect on the double about which I spoke at the end of yesterday's lecture. In the case of Ireland, the human beings who knew it in olden times described its very special characteristics in the form of fairy-tale or legend. An esoteric legend was known to express the being of Ireland within the earth's organism.

What people said was this. Once upon a time humanity was driven out of Paradise because Lucifer had led humanity astray in Paradise. So humanity was scattered across the rest of the world. The rest of the world already existed at the time when humanity was driven out of Paradise. So this legendary, fairy-tale description distinguishes between Paradise with Lucifer in it and the rest of the earth into which humanity was driven. But Ireland is different, for it does not belong to the rest of the earth in the same sense because before Lucifer entered Paradise a likeness of it came into being upon the earth, and this likeness became Ireland.

So please understand this: Ireland is that portion of the earth that has no share in Lucifer, that portion to which Lucifer has no connection. The part which had to be separated off from Paradise so that an earthly likeness could arise would have prevented Lucifer from entering into Paradise. So according to this legend Ireland was seen as the separated off part of Paradise which would have prevented Lucifer from entering into Paradise. Only when Ireland had been separated off was it possible for Lucifer to enter Paradise.

This esoteric legend which I have represented very imperfectly here is something most beautiful. For many it explained Ireland's centuries-long unique task. In the first Mystery Play I wrote, I touched on how the Christianization of Europe was started by Irish monks.[8] After Patrick had introduced Christianity to Ireland, it took on there the most deeply pious form.[9] The Greeks called Ireland 'Ierne' and the Romans 'Ivernia'. During the time when the best impulses of European Christianity emanated from Ireland, from Irish monks lovingly initiated into Christianity, the piety of Irish monasteries led to Ireland being called the Isle of Saints—as though in a new interpretation of the legend. This is linked also with the fact that the forces I mentioned, which rise up out of the earth and take hold of the human double, are of the very best kind in the island of Ireland.

You might want to say that if this is the case the very best human beings must live in Ireland. But this is not how things are in the world. Every region has migrants coming in who have descendants and so on. People are not solely the product of the one particular piece of ground they stand on. People's character might quite well contradict what rises up out of the earth. So one must not characterize a specific region of the earth's organism by pointing out what actually develops in the people there. This would be to succumb to the world of illusion.

But we can certainly say, as I have just said, that Ireland is indeed a very special location. Such a statement might provide a factor that could lead to fruitful ideas in social politics. Factors like this one I have mentioned in connection with Ireland are factors that should be reckoned with. All these things should be viewed together; there ought to be a science about the shaping of human circumstances on the earth. Before such a science comes into being there can be no really positive outcome in the way public affairs are managed. What can be said on the basis of what comes from the spiritual world ought to flow into the arrangements that are made. That is why I have been stressing in public lectures how important it is for all those who are involved in public affairs — statesmen and the like — to get to know these things.[10] Not unless they do so will they be able to take control of reality. They have not done it and are not doing it, yet it is what is necessary.

Today, in accordance with the tasks of the fifth post-Atlantean period, the important thing is to say these things, to bring them forward. Before what is said can be put into action decisions have to be taken based on impulses arising on the physical plane. This was not so in former times when matters were handled differently.

At a specific point in time during the third post-Atlantean period a certain brotherhood caused a good-sized group of people from Asia Minor to go and colonize the island of Ireland. The people who settled in Ireland came from the region of Asia where the philosopher Thales was later born.[11] You can read about the philosophy of Thales in my book *The Riddles of Philosophy*.[12] Thales hailed from the same region, but later, for he was not born until the fourth post-Atlantean period. Those initiates sent the colonists to Ireland from the same milieu, the same spiritual substance, from which the philosopher Thales later stemmed. Why? They did this because they were aware of the special characteristics of a region of the earth such as that where Ireland is situated. They knew about what is hinted at in the esoteric legend about which I spoke just now.

They knew that the forces rising up out of the earth through the soil of the island of Ireland work on human beings in such a way that they are little influenced towards becoming intellectual, little influenced towards becoming egoistic, and little influenced towards being able to take decisions firmly. The initiates who sent those colonists knew this very well, and they selected people whose karmic inclinations seemed to make them suitable for being exposed to the influences of the island of Ireland. Today there are still descendants in Ireland of that ancient population transplanted so long ago from Asia Minor who were to develop so as to have not even a trace of intellectuality, not a trace of reason, and not the ability to take firm decisions. On the other hand they were to develop special qualities of heart and soul.

Thus preparations were made beforehand for the peaceful spread of Christianity in Ireland and that glorious development of Christianity in Ireland which then spread out into the christianization of Europe. All this was prepared beforehand. Compatriots of Thales, who came later, sent people who then proved to be suited to become monks able to work in the way I have suggested. Such enterprises were frequent in olden times. So when you hear historians who do not understand this—though of course they have plenty of understanding of the kind that can be found lying in the street—when you hear these historians describing those people of ancient times, you must always be aware that such colonizations were imbued with profound wisdom. They were guided and steered always with an eye to what was to take place in the future, and account was always taken of the special characteristics of the earth's evolution.

That was a different way of bringing spiritual wisdom into the world. Nowadays those treading the right path are not permitted to act like this. They may not force people against their will to get distributed around the earth. What they have to do today is tell people the truth and it is then up to them to act.

So you see, considerable progress has taken place from the third and fourth to the fifth post-Atlanten period, and it is something of which one must be very well aware. One must realize how this impulse of freedom must run like a thread through everything that governs the fifth post-Atlantean period. It is this freedom of heart and soul which is so strongly objected to by that opponent about whom I have told you that he accompanies the human being from before birth and until death but who has to depart before death actually takes place. Under the influence of this double a great deal can emerge which is able to emerge during this fifth post-Atlantean period, a great deal which in the battle with evil is, however, not inclined to give this fifth post-Atlantean period the possibilities it needs to achieve its goal of enabling the evil to be transformed into good to some extent.

Consider, then, what must lie behind all those things in which the human beings of the fifth post-Atlantean period are involved. The correct light must be thrown on the individual facts; they must be understood. Where the double is strongly at work, that is where the true tendency of the fifth post-Atlantean period is being counteracted. But humanity in this fifth post-Atlantean period has not yet reached the point of being able to assess these facts properly. Especially in these past three sad years humanity has not been at all inclined to assess the facts at all in any proper way.

Let us look at a fact that has seemingly no connection with what I have been speaking about today. Here is the fact. At a large iron foundry, tens of thousands of tons of cast iron were to be loaded on to railway trains, and a certain number of labourers had to be employed for this purpose. It was decided to put 75 men on this job, and it turned out that they were each able to load $12\frac{1}{2}$ tons per day. So 75 men were to load $12\frac{1}{2}$ tons each per day.

There is an individual, Taylor, who is more concerned with the double than with what would promote the progress of the human heart and soul in the fifth post-Atlantean period.[13] This man asked the manufacturers whether they did not think that a single man could load much more than $12\frac{1}{2}$ tons per day. The manufacturers thought that one worker could load at most 18 tons per day. So Taylor said: Let's make an experiment.

So Taylor began to experiment with human beings, thus transferring the element of the machine into human social life. He was going to do experiments with human beings! He tested whether what those most practically minded manufacturers said was true: whether one man could really load only 18 tons per day. He introduced rest breaks calculated physiologically to allow for the recoupment of as much energy as had been expended. Of course it became obvious that this varied from person to person. As you know, such variation cannot be applied to mechanical procedures; you have to take the arithmetical average. But with human beings you cannot take the arithmetical average because every individual has a right to his own existence. But Taylor took the arithmetical average. He selected those workers whose break times overall were economical, and these economical break times were allowed. The others, who could not recoup their strength in these break times were simply thrown out. In human experiments like these it turned out that if you selected those workers who recovered fully in the allotted breaks, then every man was able to load $47\frac{1}{2}$ tons.

Thus the mechanism of Darwin's theory is applied to the life of working men: throw out those who do not fit, select those who do.[14] Those who fit are the ones who can load not 18 tons, as had previously been thought, but $47\frac{1}{2}$ tons when given the required rest breaks. This also makes it possible to satisfy the workers' wishes because when a lot of money is saved their wages can be increased by 60 per cent. So the ones who are selected, the ones who are best fitted for the struggle for existence can, in addition, be turned into very satisfied fellows. But the ones who do not fit might as well starve!

This is how a principle is born! Little note is taken of such things because they are not examined in the light of wider perspectives. But one must examine them in the light of wider perspectives. Today this is nothing more than an erroneous application of scientific ideas to human life. But the impulse is there. And then it begins to be applied to those things that make their appearance as esoteric truths during the fifth post-Atlantean period. There is nothing esoteric in Darwinism. Nevertheless, if it were to be applied more widely it would lead to much frightfulness, namely, if it were to be applied to direct experimentation with human beings. If the esoteric truths that must be revealed during the course of the fifth post-Atlantean period were to be added, though, then one would gain immense power over people merely through always selecting the most suitable. But it would not remain merely a matter of selecting the most suitable, for by striving to achieve a certain occult invention that would make the most suitable ever more and more suitable one would achieve immense power that would work counter to the good tendencies of the fifth post-Atlantean period.

I wanted to show you how these things hang together in order to demonstrate what the early beginnings of wider intentions for the future look like and why it is necessary to throw light on them from a higher perspective.

Next time it will be our task to point out the three or four great truths which must be arrived at by the fifth post-Atlantean period. We shall show how these truths can be misused if they are not applied in the sense of the right and good tendencies of the fifth post-Atlantean period but instead are made to fulfil the conditions of the double, conditions represented by those brotherhoods who want to replace Christ by another being.

7. Individual Spirit Beings and the Constant Foundation of the Universe, III

In order to expand on them I shall today refer back to some of the points we have been considering. For long ages human beings have had thoughts, feelings and impulses to help them find whatever they needed to make progress. But now the signs of the times are telling us that these thoughts, feelings and impulses no longer give us what we require to help us go towards the near future.

Yesterday one of our members showed me last Wednesday's issue of the *Frankfurter Zeitung*.[1] In it there is an article by a very learned gentleman; indeed he must be exceedingly learned, for his name is preceded by the letters denoting not only Doctor of Philosophy but also those denoting Doctor of Theology, and these are in turn preceded by the title of Professor. So this man is very clever indeed. His essay is about all kinds of modern spiritual needs, and it contains the following passage: '*The experience of the beingness* that lies behind everything requires neither pious solemnity nor religious evaluation, for it is, in itself, *religion*. It is not one's own individual content that must be sensed and grasped, but the grand irrationality that lies hidden behind all existence. Those who touch it and cause the divine spark to flash across will undergo an experience that is primeval and prototypical. This unites the one who is having the experience with all that moves in the same stream of life; he is vouchsafed a cosmic sense of life — to use a favourite phrase of recent times.'

Forgive me, dear friends. I am not reading this to you in order to awaken any great ideas that might be contained in these wishy-washy sentences but in order to demonstrate a sign of the times: 'A *cosmic religiosity* is in the making among us, and the strength of people's longing for it is demonstrated by the perceptible growth of the *theosophical* movement which is attempting to discover and reveal the gyrations of that hidden life.' It isn't easy to stumble through all these wishy-washy concepts, but they are, are they not, remarkable as signs of the times! The writer continues: 'This cosmic piety is not a matter of quietistic mysticism that begins with a rejection of the world and ends in contemplation for it is received among the rolling waves of events and arouses ever new commotion' — and so on.

It really is not possible to make any sense of all this! But since it is preceded by 'Professor, DD and D.Phil.' we must surely regard it as something clever, for otherwise we should have to see in it the stammerings and unclear ramblings of a learned gentleman who cannot discern the way forward on the path he is following but nonetheless feels obliged to hint at something which does exist and which appears to him to be not entirely without hope.

We ought not to find anything pleasing in such outpourings, for such outpourings must above all not be allowed to lull us to sleep in the pleasant notion that here, once again, is someone who has noticed that there is, after all, something worthwhile behind the spiritual science movement. It would be very damaging if this were to happen. For those who express such outpourings are sometimes the very ones who feel satisfied by them but who do not press on. In their wishy-washy way they point to something that wants to enter into the world yet they remain much, much too idle to embark on any serious study of spiritual science and of what it is that must take hold of human hearts and souls if these realities are to enter the stream of coming existence in ways that will be beneficial. It is of course easier to talk of 'rolling waves' and 'cosmic feelings' than it is to go more seriously into things which — as the signs of the times demand — must be told to humanity just now. That is why it seems necessary to me to say here what I said and will continue to say in the public lectures,[2] while emphasizing the difference between what is dead and gone with no life left in it but which has led us into the present catastrophic times, and what the human soul must really grasp if any kind of forward step is to be taken.

You could hold thousands of congresses, world congresses and peoples' congresses or whatever, involving the old wisdom which has brought humanity thus far; and thousands and thousands of societies could be founded. But it must be clearly understood that these thousands of congresses and thousands of societies will achieve nothing if the spiritual life-blood of the science of the spirit does not flow through them.

What people lack today is the courage to embark properly on researching the spiritual world. Strange though it may sound, it has to be said that a next step could simply be to spread the booklet *Approaches to Anthroposophy* in the widest circles.[3] That would be another way of bringing forward knowledge about the links between human beings and the cosmic order. The booklet draws attention to this knowledge. Attention is drawn to actual facts, such as the way in which the earth changes its states of consciousness year by year. What is said in the lecture and in the booklet is said expressly with the needs of our time in mind. To absorb this would mean more than all that wishy-washy talk of cosmic feelings or mingling with some 'rolling waves' of whatever kind. I have just read these things aloud to you and I cannot repeat them because they are too meaningless in the way they are formulated.

This does not mean that we must not pay attention to these things, for they are important and real. I want to make it clear, though, that we must not create our own fog but should always retain the utmost clarity if we want to work for the spiritual science of anthroposophy.

Once again I want to remind you that during this fifth post-Atlantean period the time is approaching when humanity will be having to deal very carefully with certain great life questions that have thus far been hidden, in a way, by the wisdom of former times. I have already pointed this out.[4] One of these great life questions can be described as follows. Endeavours are to be undertaken to place the spiritually etheric element in the service of external, practical life. I have already pointed out that the fifth post-Atlantean period will have to solve the problem of how the temper of the human soul, the flow of human moods, can be transmitted to machines in wavelike movements.[5] The human being must be linked with something that has to grow more and more mechanical. A week ago I spoke of the external way in which a certain part of our earth is taking this mechanization.[6] I gave the example of how the American way of thinking is trying to spread mechanical principles to include human life itself. I spoke of the rest-breaks that are to be used to enable a specific number of workers to load not fewer tons but up to 50 tons. All that is needed for this is to introduce Darwin's principle of selection into life.

At such places there is the will to harness human energy with mechanical energy. It would be quite wrong to think that we should try to prevent these things, for they will happen, they will come about. The only question is whether they will be brought about as a part of human evolution by people who are selflessly familiar with the great goals of earthly evolution and will do them in ways that are beneficial to humanity or whether they will be brought about by those groups of people who only want to make use of them egoistically or solely for the sake of their own group. It is not 'what' is done that matters in this instance, for the 'what' will happen anyway; the important thing here is the 'how', how these things are tackled. The 'what' will happen anyway because it is intrinsic in earthly evolution. Welding together human nature with mechanical nature will be a great and significant ongoing problem for the remainder of earthly evolution.

Recently I have often very deliberately pointed out, also in public lectures, that human consciousness is linked with the forces of destruction. Twice in public lectures in Basle I have said: 'We die into our nervous system.'[7] These forces, these forces of dying away will grow ever stronger and stronger. Connections will be created between the human being's forces of dying away—which are related to electrical, to magnetic forces—and external mechanical forces. People will be able in a certain way to steer their intentions and their thoughts into the mechanical forces. As yet undiscovered forces in the human being will be discovered, forces that work on external electrical and magnetic forces.

That is the one question: the linking of the human being with mechanisms, this being something that will gain ground more and more in the future. Another problem is the matter of calling on spiritual conditions for help. This will only be possible when the time is ripe and when a sufficient number of individuals will have been prepared for this in the right way. But it must happen eventually that the spiritual forces are mobilized to have control over life in relation to sickness and death.

Medicine will be made spiritual, very, very spiritual. But caricatures of this will also be created by a certain quarter. These caricatures, however, will only serve to show what must actually come about in reality. Once again, as with the other problem, this matter will be taken up in an external, egoistic way by individuals or groups.

A third matter is the introduction of human thinking into how the human race comes into being through birth and conception. I have pointed out that congresses about this have already been set up, and also that in future there will be a materialistic elaboration of the science concerned with conception and how man and woman are harnessed together.[8] All these things point to significant developments. Today it is still all too easy to ask why those who know about these things in the right way do not put them into practice.

In future it will be possible to reach an understanding of what is involved in the practical application of these things and to see what forces are still at work just now putting obstacles in the way of developing a spiritualized science of medicine, for example, or of economics. One cannot do more today than speak about these things until people have understood them sufficiently, those individuals, namely, who will want to take them up in a selfless way. Many believe they can already do these things; but many life factors still prevent such a thing, and these can only be overcome by allowing an ever deeper understanding to gain ground and by renouncing, for a while at least, any direct efforts at practical application on a larger scale.

In all these matters it has to be said that not much remains now of whatever existed behind the old, atavistic endeavours carried on up to the fourteenth or fifteenth centuries. Today people talk a lot about ancient alchemy, remembering the process of producing the homunculus and so on. Most of what is said misses the mark. A time will come when people will understand what is meant by the Homunculus scene in Goethe's *Faust.*[9] But since the sixteenth century these things have been shrouded in mist; awareness of them has receded.

The law governing these things is the same law that determines the rhythmical alternation of waking and sleeping in the human being. Just as a human being cannot disregard sleep, so could humanity, where spiritual development is concerned, not avoid the sleep in matters of spiritual science that characterizes the centuries since the sixteenth century. Humanity had to go to sleep spiritually so that spirituality could reappear in a new form. One simply has to come to terms with such necessities. But we must not be downcast about them. We must realize that the time has now come to wake up, that we can participate in working at this awakening, that events often precede knowledge, and that we will fail to comprehend the events going on all around us if we do not make the effort to gain the knowledge.

I have repeatedly mentioned that certain groups of people working in egoistically occult ways are making efforts in certain directions. Initially it was necessary for a specific kind of knowledge to retire into the background for humanity—knowledge nowadays given incomprehensible names such as alchemy or astrology and so on. This knowledge had to disappear, be slept through, so that people no longer had the possibility of drawing soul qualities out of their observations of nature but were instead more thrown back on themselves. So that human beings could awaken the forces of their own being it was necessary for certain matters to appear first in an abstract form which must now take on a concrete spiritual form.

Three ideas have gradually been given form over the course of recent centuries, ideas that are abstract in the way they have come amongst human beings. Kant wrongly called them: God, freedom and immortality.[10] Goethe rightly called them: God, virtue and immortality.[11]

What is encompassed by these three words is now rather abstract, whereas in the fourteenth or fifteenth century it was more concrete, but in the old atavistic sense also more physical. People experimented in the old way, endeavouring in alchemical experiments to observe processes that revealed the working of God. They tried to produce the philosophers' stone.

There is something concrete behind all these things. The philosophers' stone was supposed to help the human being become virtuous, although this was thought of in a more material sense. It was also intended that it should make people able to experience immortality by placing themselves in a relationship with the cosmos that would let them experience what lies beyond birth and death. All the wishy-washy ideas people use today in their effort to grasp these things no longer fit with what was striven for in those days. Things have become abstract, and modern humanity talks about abstract ideas. People try to comprehend God by means of abstract theology, and virtue, too, as something wholly abstract. The more abstract the idea, the more does modern humanity like talking about these things. The same goes for immortality. People speculate about what could be immortal in the human being. In the first Basle lecture I spoke of today's science of philosophy being a starved science, an undernourished science in the way it deals with questions such as immortality.[12] This is only a different description of the abstract way in which these things are striven for nowadays.

Certain brotherhoods of the West, however, have preserved the connection with the old traditions and are trying to apply it in ways that will place it at the service of a kind of group egoism. These things must be pointed out. Of course, when this quarter in the West mentions these things in public, exoteric literature it also talks of God, virtue or freedom, and immortality in the abstract sense. But those in the circles of initiates know that all this is speculation and that it is all abstract. Amongst themselves they look for something much more concrete in the abstract formulations of God, virtue and immortality. So in the schools in question these words are translated for the initiates.

God is translated as gold, and they seek to fathom the question of the mystery of gold. For gold—the representative of what is sunlike within the earth's crust—is indeed something that embodies an important secret. In the material sense, gold relates to other substances as the thought of God relates to other thoughts. The crucial thing is how this mystery is interpreted.

This is connected with the way these groups egoistically make use of the mystery of birth. They try to attain a genuinely cosmic understanding. But in recent times human beings have replaced this cosmic understanding with an understanding that is totally earthly. If they want to study how, for example, the embryo of an animal or human being develops, they point their microscope at what is present at the location on the earth where they are looking through that microscope. They regard this as the thing they should be studying. But this cannot be the case. They will discover—and certain circles are very near to making this discovery—that the forces at work are not to be found in what they are examining through their microscope but that these forces come in from the cosmos, from the constellation in the cosmos. When an embryo comes into being, it comes into being because cosmic forces streaming from all the directions of the cosmos are at work in the living creature inside which the embryo is forming. What will arise when fertilization takes place will depend on which cosmic forces are active during the fertilization.

Something will have to be understood which is not understood as yet. Suppose you have a living creature, a hen, shall we say. When a new life arises within this living creature, the biologist focuses his observation on how the egg is growing out of the hen. He investigates the forces that he supposes are making the egg grow out of the hen herself. This is nonsense. The egg does not grow out of the hen for she is merely the foundation. Forces ray in from the cosmos and generate the egg on the ground prepared for it within the hen. But the biologist imagines that the forces in question are situated at the spot he is examining through his microscope, whereas what he is seeing is something that depends on the forces of the stars working together in a specific constellation at a certain spot. The truth of the matter will only be discovered when the cosmic forces are discovered, namely, that it is the cosmos that conjures the egg into the hen.

All these things are connected above all with the mystery of the sun, and from the earthly point of view with the mystery of gold. What I am putting forward today is no more than a schematic hint, but as time goes on these matters will become much clearer.

In the schools that have been mentioned virtue is not

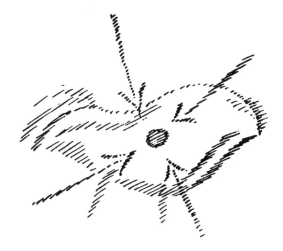

spoken of as virtue but as health. Here the endeavour is to find out what cosmic constellations are involved when human beings recover their health or fall ill. By getting to know the cosmic constellations one also finds out about the different substances in the earth's surface, fluids and so on, that are in their turn linked to health and sickness. From a particular quarter a more material form of health science will be developed which will, however, rest on a spiritualistic foundation.

The concept to be disseminated from that quarter is that people do not become good through learning all kinds of ethical principles in the abstract but through taking, let us say, copper under a specific constellation, or arsenic under another constellation. You can imagine how these things can be utilized for the egoistic intentions of certain groups to gain power! Simply by not disseminating such knowledge to others, who are then prevented from participating, one has at one's disposal the best means of controlling great masses of the population. Without making any mention of something like this one could, for example, introduce a new kind of snack. This new snack, duly adulterated, could then be marketed. Such things can be done when one conceives of these matters in a materialistic way. One must simply be aware that everything material is filled with the workings of spirituality. Only those who know that in the true sense of the word nothing material exists, but only what is spiritual, can plumb the mysteries of life.

In a similar vein there is the matter of bringing the question of immortality into materialistic channels. This matter of immortality can be brought into materialistic channels in similar ways, by utilizing the cosmic con-stellations. This does not lead to the attainment of what is often speculated to be immortality, but it does bring about another kind of immortality. Since it is not yet possible to work on the physical body as a way of artificially extending life, one prepares to undergo certain experiences in the soul that will enable one to remain within the lodge of brothers even after death when one can help out with the forces that are then at one's disposal. So in those circles immortality is referred to simply as life-extension.

Outward signs of all this are already to be seen. Perhaps some of you noticed the book *Der Unfug des Sterbens* (Death is a nonsense) that came over from the West and made quite a sensation for a time.[13] Such things are all pointing in that direction, but they are only a beginning, for anything that reaches beyond the beginning is still being stored up for egoistic group activities and kept as something very eso-teric. These things are possible if they are brought into materialistic channels, if the abstract ideas of God, virtue and immortality are turned into the concrete ideas of gold, health and life-extension, if the great questions of the fifth post-Atlantean period I mentioned earlier are used to further the purposes of group egoism.

What that Professor and Doctor of Theology and Doctor of Philosophy wishy-washily termed 'cosmic feeling' is already being presented by many — also unfortunately in many cases in an egoistic sense — as the cosmic knowledge of the human being. Whereas for centuries science has paid attention only to things that work side by side on the earth and has avoided any glance towards the most important element that comes in from outside the earth, what will happen now in the fifth post-Atlantean period is that specifically those forces which come in from the cosmos will be put to use. And just as the most important thing for biology professors now is to have microscopes that provide the greatest possible degree of enlargement and laboratory procedures that are most appropriate, in future, when science has become spiritual, the important thing will be whether certain processes are put in train in the morning or the evening, or at midday; or whether what one has done in the morning can be further influenced by what works in the evening or whether it excludes or paralyses the cosmic influence of the morning until the evening.

Of course much water will still flow down the Rhine before the purely materialistic platforms, laboratories and suchlike are handed over to spiritual scientists. But if humanity wants to avoid sinking into complete decadence the work of these laboratories will have to be replaced by another kind of work. For example, in the case of the good that should be attained in the immediate future, certain processes take place in the morning and are then interrupted during the rest of the day. Then in the evening the cosmic streams flow through them again, and the result is then rhythmically preserved until the next morning. In this way processes take place in which certain cosmic effects are always interrupted during the day and introduced during the morning and the evening. This will call for all kinds of different ways of doing things.

From all this it will be obvious to you that if one is not in a position to take part publicly in these things then all one can do is to speak about them. Those quarters that want to replace God, virtue and immortality with gold, health and life-extension are the very quarters which strive to work with forces that are quite different from the forces of morning and evening processes. I mentioned last time that a certain quarter seeks to remove the impulse of the Mystery of Golgotha from the world by bringing in another impulse from the West, a kind of Antichrist, and that coming from the East the Christ-impulse as it appears in the twentieth century is to be paralysed by distracting people's attention from the coming of Christ in the etheric realm.

From the quarter which will put forward the Antichrist as the Christ will come endeavours to make use of something that can work through the most material of forces, something that can work spiritually through the most material of forces. More than anything else, that quarter will strive to make use of electricity, especially the earth's magnetism, to bring about effects all over the world. I have shown you how the forces of the earth rise up in what I have termed the human double.[14] People will discover this secret. It will be an American secret to use the earth's magnetism in its duality, the northern and southern magnetism, in order to send controlling forces across the whole earth, forces that work spiritually. Look at the magnetic map of the earth and compare the magnetic map with what I am about to say, namely, the magnetic line where the needle deflects to the east and to the west, and where it does not deflect at all. I cannot now give more than hints about these things.

Spiritual beings are incessantly working in from a specific point of the compass. All that needs to be done is to get these spiritual beings to work in the service of earth existence; and then, since those beings working in from the cosmos are able to mediate the secret of the earth's magnetism, one will be able to fathom that secret. Thereafter, with regard to those three things — gold, health and life-extension — one will be able to work very effectively in the direction of group egoism. It will be a matter of mustering the dubious courage to do these things. And within certain circles this courage will surely be mustered!

Coming from the direction of the east it will be a matter of strengthening what I have already described by also placing in the service of the earth those beings who are streaming down from the opposite direction of the cosmos. There will be a great struggle in the future. Human science will turn to cosmic influences, but it will endeavour to do so in various ways. The task of good, beneficial science will be to find certain cosmic forces that can come into being on the earth through the working together of two cosmic streams arriving from different directions. These two cosmic streams from different directions will be Pisces and Virgo. It will above all be a matter of discovering how what works as sun forces from the cosmos coming from Pisces can combine with what works from the direction of Virgo. This is what will be good: to discover how from two directions of the cosmos morning and evening forces can be placed in the service of humanity, those coming from the direction of Pisces and those coming from the direction of Virgo.

These forces will be of no interest to those who endeavour to achieve everything by means of the dualism of polarity,

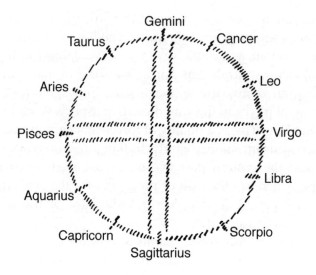

through positive and negative forces. The spiritual secrets that on earth can cause the spirit to stream through from the cosmos—with the help of the dual forces of positive and negative magnetism—these spiritual secrets derive from the direction of Gemini. They are the forces of midday. Even in ancient times it was known that this is something cosmic, and scientists today know exoterically that behind Gemini in the zodiac positive and negative magnetism exists in some way.

Here it will be a matter of paralysing what should be won from the cosmos through the revelation of duality, a matter of paralysing this in a materialistic, egoistic way through the forces that stream to humanity especially from Gemini, forces that can be put to work entirely in the service of the double.

Then there are the brotherhoods who want to bypass the Mystery of Golgotha. They will make use of the human being's dual nature which, now in the fifth post-Atlantean period, contains on the one hand the human being and on the other the lower, animal nature. The human being truly is a centaur in a certain way, for he contains the lower animal nature astrally, and in a way the human part is simply grafted on to this animal nature. Here again we have a duality of forces in the way these two aspects work in the human being. This is a duality of forces that certain egoistic brotherhoods in a more easterly, Indian direction will use to lead also the eastern part of Europe astray, that part of Europe which has the task of preparing for the sixth post-Atlantean period. This dualism makes use of the forces coming from Sagittarius.

What lies in store for humanity is that the cosmic forces will be won for humanity in a dual way that is wrong or a single way that is right. This will bring a genuine renewal to astrology, which is atavistic in its old form—a form in which it cannot continue to exist. Those who know about the cosmos will struggle against one another. Some will make use of the morning and evening processes in the way I have suggested; in the West the midday processes will mostly be used while the morning and evening processes are excluded, and in the East the midnight processes will be used. It will no longer be a matter of making substances only according to the chemical processes of attraction and repulsion, for people will know that the substance will be different depending on whether it is produced by means of morning and evening processes or by midday and midnight processes. They will know that such substances work quite differently on the trinity of God, virtue and immortality, or gold, health and life-extension.

It will not be possible to achieve anything bad by means of a collaboration between what comes from Pisces and Virgo. What will be achieved through these will, it is true, detach the mechanism of life somewhat from the human being, but it will not be a foundation for any kind of power or dominion of one group over another. The cosmic forces brought in from this direction will produce remarkable machines, machines that can be labour-saving for people because they will contain a degree of intelligence. And it will be the task of a science of the spirit concerned with the cosmos to ensure that all the great temptations emanating from these machine-animals created by human beings themselves will be unable to have any damaging influence on them.

Something important must be said in connection with all this. It is essential to prepare for it all by no longer assuming that realities are illusions and by really entering into a spiritual view of the world and gaining a spiritual grasp of the world. Much depends on seeing things for what they are! But we can only see them for what they are if we are able to apply to reality the concepts and ideas given to us by the spiritual science of anthroposophy.

For the remainder of earthly existence the dead will collaborate with us to a high degree. But *how* they collaborate will be what matters, for there will be great differences. It will be important that people on the earth behave in such a way that collaboration with the dead in a good way can be allowed to be guided by them, so that the impulse coming from them is the starting-point coming from the spiritual world which the dead themselves experience after death.

There will also, on the other hand, be many attempts to introduce the dead into human life by artificial means. The dead will be brought into human life via a detour through Gemini which in quite a specific way will cause human vibrations to continue resonating in the machines. The cosmos will then move the machines via the detour I have just mentioned.

If these problems arise it will be important to use nothing improper but only those elemental forces derived from nature itself; one must not introduce any improper forces into the life of these machines. In this occult field one must not harness the human being to the mechanism in any way that makes use of the Darwinistic theory of selection in connection with human labour as in the example I gave last time.

I am giving you all these hints, which cannot of course exhaust the subject in such a short time, because I am sure you will continue to mull them over and endeavour to build a bridge between them and your own life experiences, especially those we are gaining today in these difficult times. You will see how much clarity you will gain when you look at things in the light of these ideas. It is not a matter now of a confrontation between forces and con-stellations of forces about which so much is being said in external, exoteric life, for it is a matter of quite other things. What is happening now is that a kind of veil is being drawn over the true impulses we are concerned with. Human forces are at work trying to garner something for them-selves. What do they want to garner? Certain human forces are at work defending the impulses that were justifiable impulses up to the time of the French Revolution and were then also represented by certain secret schools; but now the endeavour is to represent them in a retarded, ahrimanic-luciferic form in a way that would maintain a social order thought to have been overcome by humanity since the end of the eighteenth century.

In the main there are two camps in opposition to one another: the representatives of the principle that had been overcome by the end of the eighteenth century, and the representatives of the present time. Of course a great number of people instinctively represent the impulses of the present time. So those who are supposed to represent the old impulses of the eighteenth, seventeenth, sixteenth centuries will have to be harnessed by artificial means emanating from certain brotherhoods working to promote their group egoism. The most effective principle of modern times that can be used to extend one's power over the number of people one wishes to use is the economic principle, the principle of economic dependence. But this is merely the tool. The real concern is something quite different. The real concern is what you will have surmised from all the hints I have been giving. The economic principle is connected with all that can be used to make a huge number of people across the earth into a kind of army for these principles.

These are the matters that confront one another, the ones that are really doing battle in the world today. Rooted in the West there is the principle of the eighteenth, seventeenth, sixteenth centuries which makes itself invisible by clothing itself in the phrases of the Revolution, the phrases of democracy, the principle which dons this mask and is striving to gain as much power as possible. It is advantageous for this principle if as many individuals as possible make no effort to see things as they really are and constantly allow themselves to be lulled by *maya*, the *maya* that is expressed in the words: There is a war going on between the Entente and the Central Powers.

In reality there is no such war, and our concern should be for quite other things that are the true reality behind the *maya*. The battle of the Entente with the Central Powers is merely an illusion. We can reach a conclusion about what is really doing battle if we look behind things and illumine them in the way I am, for certain reasons, only hinting at. One must at least try for oneself not to mistake illusion for reality, and then the illusion will gradually dissolve as far as is necessary. One must try above all to see things as they show themselves to a realistic and unprejudiced view.

If you look at all the things I have been unfolding here, you will find that even a remark I made on the side during these lectures was not as unimportant as it might have seemed.[15] When I said that a remark made by Mephistopheles to Faust, 'I see that thou the Devil knowest,'[16] would not have been made by him to Woodrow Wilson,[17] this was not an unimportant observation. It was in fact intended to throw light on the situation! One must be able to look at these things without either sympathy or antipathy; they must be seen objectively. One must consider what constellations signify in something that is at work, and what a person's own forces signify. Frequently something entirely different lies behind a person's own forces than what lies behind the mere constellation. Ask yourselves objectively what the value of Woodrow Wilson's brain would be if this brain did not happen to be seated upon the presidential chair of the North American Union. Assume that this brain were situated in a different constellation: that is where it would reveal its own personal force! So it is the constellation that matters.

Let me put it in the abstract and radically, although not to illustrate the instance I have just mentioned, for I would not do such a thing in this very neutral country. Apart from that instance, consider the important insight that would be revealed if one were to ask whether a certain brain attained its value through being illuminated spiritually in a special way, in the sense I have been describing in these lectures, or whether its value scarcely exceeded the result obtained by placing it in a scale and balancing it against weights in the other scale.

The moment you penetrate fully into all the secrets of the double, whom I mentioned last time, you will find yourself able to assess the value of brains that are merely lumps which you have placed on a scale, lumps which can be brought to life solely by the double.

All these things appear grotesque to people today, but everything that is grotesque about them must come to be seen as perfectly ordinary if certain matters are to be guided from harmful into beneficial channels. There is no point in constantly talking round them! You must come to realize that all the wishy-washy talk of 'cosmic religiosity' or 'how powerful the yearning for it is' or 'the movement that is undertaking to discover and unveil the circulations of life not accessible to the senses' and so on is also nothing other than a means of spreading fog over these matters which ought actually to be entering the world in clarity, which can only work in clarity and which, above all, ought only to be carried in clarity into human life as practical moral and ethical impulses.

I can only bring you certain isolated hints. So now I leave it to your own meditation to build further in these matters. Much is aphoristic. But if you take summaries such as the zodiac I have drawn here (see p. 190) and really use it as material for meditation you will be able to derive a very great deal from them.

Notes

These lectures were originally taken down in German shorthand and afterwards immediately rewritten in longhand by the professional stenographer Helene Finckh. The drawings within the text were done by Assya Turgeniev and Leonore Uhlig after sketches produced by the stenographer.

Lecture 1

1 Nicolaus Copernicus (1473–1543). Polish astronomer, mathematician, physician, jurist, humanist and cleric. Propounded the heliocentric view of the universe. He was on his deathbed when *De revolutionibus orbium coelestium libri VI*, which he had dedicated to Pope Paul III, was published. In the foreword, written by his friend and publisher, the method of calculation was declared to be purely hypothetical and scientific. The work thus slipped past the censor until it came to be banned at its third edition in 1616/17. The Catholic Church did not accept its content until 1822. See *inter alia* R. Steiner, *The Spiritual Guidance of the Individual and Humanity* (GA 15), Anthroposophic Press, New York 1992, lecture III.

2 See Note 20.

3 R. Steiner, *The Case for Anthroposophy*, Rudolf Steiner Press, London 1970 (extracts from *Von Seelenrätseln*, GA 21, Dornach 1984).

4 Friedrich Theodor Vischer (1807–87). Aesthete and poet. 'Der Traum. Eine Studie zu der Schrift *Die Traumphantasie* von Dr. Joh. Volkelt', in *Altes und Neues*, 3 issues in one volume, Stuttgart 1881–82; 1st issue, Stuttgart 1881.

5   Johannes Volkelt (1848–1930). Professor of Philosophy at Leipzig. *Die Traumphantasie*, Stuttgart 1875.

6   F. T. Vischer, op. cit. p. 194, literally: '... the soul, as the supreme unifier of all processes, cannot be situated within the body, yet it is not elsewhere than in the body.'

7   Emil Du Bois-Reymond (1818–96). Two lectures in Leipzig published as *Über die Grenzen des Naturerkennens. Die sieben Welträtsel.*

8   F. T. Vischer, op. cit. p. 229.

9   R. Steiner, *How to Know Higher Worlds* (GA 10), Anthroposophic Press, Hudson 1994.

10   R. Steiner, *An Outline of Esoteric Science* (GA 13), Anthroposophic Press, Hudson 1997. By 'second part' the speaker means the chapter 'Knowledge of Higher Worlds — Initiation'.

11   See descriptions of the various world views in R. Steiner, *Human and Cosmic Thought* (GA 151), Rudolf Steiner Press, London 1967.

12   James Dewar (1842–1923). Physicist and chemist, professor in Cambridge and London. Inventor of the thermos flask. A record of the lecture given by Dewar at the Royal Institution has not been found. A précis in German is given by Carl Snyder in *Das Weltbild der modernen Naturwissenschaft nach den Ergebnissen der heutigen Forschung*, Leipzig 1905. See also R. Steiner, *The Foundations of Human Experience* (GA 293,66), Anthroposophic Press, Hudson 1996, lecture of 22 March 1917; and *Freiheit – Unsterblichkeit – Soziales Leben* (GA 72), Dornach 1990, lecture of 19 October 1917.

13   Wilhelm Carl Röntgen (1845–1923). Discovered X-rays in 1895. Awarded the Nobel Prize for physics in 1901.

14   Derived from the theories of Immanuel Kant (1724–1804) and Pierre Simon Laplace (1749–1824) regarding the nebular origins of the universe.

15   R. Steiner, *The Riddle of Man* (GA 20), Mercury Press, Spring Valley 1990, especially his remarks about Karl Christian

Planck (p. 60ff.) and Robert Hamerling (p. 112ff.) and on both these individuals in the chapter 'New Perspectives'.

16   See Notes 9 and 10.

17   See R. Steiner, *The Riddle of Man*, op. cit., the chapter 'New Perspectives'.

18   Rudolf Steiner described the faculties of Imagination (forming meaningful inner images), Inspiration (hearing inwardly what is at the heart of things) and Intuition (knowing beings and things through 'living into' them) as a further development of thinking, feeling and will. See R. Steiner, *The Stages of Higher Knowledge* (GA 12), Anthroposophic Press, New York 1967.

19   R. Steiner used the term 'formative-forces body' to describe the ether body for the first time in January 1917 in the second part of his essay 'Die Erkenntnis vom Zustand zwischen dem Tode und einer neuen Geburt', in *Philosophie und Anthroposophie. Gesammelte Aufsätze 1904–1923* (GA 35), Dornach 1984. See also the footnote on 'ether body or life body' in part 4 of Chapter 1, and the Addendum to the same page, in *Theosophy* (GA 9), Rudolf Steiner Press, London 1970.

20   Charles Darwin (1809–82). Scientist, physician, geologist, botanist: *On the Origin of Species by means of Natural Selection*, 1859.

21   Ernst Haeckel (1834–1919). German zoologist and scientist. See *inter alia* his book *The Natural History of Creation, Part 2; Anthropogenie* (History of human development); *The Riddle of the Universe* (A study of monistic philosophy).

22   Eduard von Hartmann (1842–1906). German philosopher. Wrote *The Philosophy of the Unconscious*.

23   The anonymous paper was in fact by Hartmann himself and was later (1877) published under his name in a second edition.

24   In the Foreword to the fourth edition (1873) of his *Natural History of Creation*: 'This excellent paper says essentially everything I myself might have said about *The Philosophy of the Unconscious* . . .'

25   Oscar Hertwig (1849–1922). German anatomist, pupil of
     Ernst Haeckel: *Das Werden der Organismen. Eine Widerlegung
     von Darwins Zufallstheorie* (Evolution of organisms. A refu-
     tation of Darwin's theory of chance), Jena 1916.
26   Ibid., Postscript, p. 710.
27   See R. Steiner, *Nature's Open Secret. Introductions to Goethe's
     Scientific Writings* (in GA 1a–e), Anthroposophic Press,
     Hudson 2000. See also R. Steiner, *Goethe's World View* (GA 6),
     Mercury Press, Spring Valley, NY 1985.
28   The wooden, double-domed first Goetheanum. See: W.
     Roggenkamp, *Das Goetheanum als Gesamtkunstwerk* with R.
     Steiner's lecture of 29 June 1921, Dornach 1986.
29   R. Steiner, *Nature's Open Secret*, op. cit.
30   Albrecht von Haller (1708–77). Swiss physician, botanist and
     poet.
31   Goethe, 'True Enough: *To the Physicist*', as translated by
     Michael Hamburger in *Poems* and quoted in *Goethe, Scientific
     Studies* (ed. & tr. by D. Miller), Suhrkamp Publishers, New
     York 1988.
32   J. W. von Goethe, 'Wer Wissenschaft und Kunst besitzt', in
     Gedichte, 3. Teil. Deutsche National-Litteratur (tr. J.C.).

Lecture 2

1   Lecture 1 in the present volume.
2   On R. Steiner's statements regarding the problem of pub-
     lishing esoteric material, see W. Kugler's collection in *Beiträge
     zur Rudolf Steiner Gesamtausgabe* No. 105, Michaelmas 1990,
     p. 39ff.
3   On the evolutionary epochs and much else see R. Steiner,
     Cosmic Memory (GA 11), Rudolf Steiner Publications, New
     York 1971; and *An Outline of Esoteric Science*, op. cit., especially
     the chapter 'Cosmic Evolution and the Human Being'.
4   Paul, 1 Corinthians, 1,20: '... hath not God made foolish the
     wisdom of this world', and 3,19: 'For the wisdom of this
     world is foolishness with God.'

5   See *inter alia* R. Steiner, *Cosmic Memory*, op. cit.; *An Outline of Esoteric Science*, op. cit., chapter 'Cosmic Evolution and the Human Being'; and *The Spiritual Hierarchies and the Physical World* (GA 110, 132), Anthroposophic Press, Hudson 1996.

6   See Lecture 4 in the present volume and R. Steiner, *Die Ergänzung heutiger Wissenschaften durch Anthroposophie* (GA 73), Dornach 1987, lecture of 14 Novemer 1917.

7   Paracelsus, Theophrastus von Hohenheim (1493–1541). German physician, scientist and philosopher. City physician and professor at the University of Basle.

8   Columban (*c*. 550–615). The Irish monk who from 595 travelled with twelve pupils (including St Gall) as a missionary through Franconia, Burgundy, Alemania and Lombardy.

9   St Gall (of Hibernia) (550/555–641 or 645). Pupil who accompanied Columban on his missionary journey and remained behind as a hermit in the hills above the Lake of Constance.

10   See Lecture 1 in the present volume.

11   Ralph Waldo Emerson (1803–82), American philosopher and essayist.

12   Woodrow Wilson (1856–1924). President of the USA (1912–20).

13   See R. Steiner, *Die Ergänzung heutiger Wissenschaften durch Anthroposophie*, op. cit., lecture of 7 November 1917.

14   For example in R. Steiner, *The Influence of Spiritual Beings upon Man* (in GA 102), Anthroposophic Press, New York 1961, lecture of 11 June 1908.

15   Sophie Stinde (1853–1915). See R. Steiner on Sophie Stinde in *Unsere Toten. Ansprachen, Gedenkworte und Meditationssprüche 1906–1924* (GA 261), Dornach 1984.

16   At this point the lecturer spoke as follows (see also Note 10 to Lecture 4): 'Unfortunately I am obliged to conclude our considerations here by adding that the work of the anthroposophical movement is not only meeting with resistance and prejudice today, but that recently defamation and slan-

der have been strongly asserting themselves as well. On account of this, because this defamation is specifically linked to my personal conversations with individual members of our Society, I have decided with a heavy heart to cut down on these personal conversations about people's esoteric life. The defamations perpetrated by members not authorized to speak about such things — but I do not wish to go into detail here — are such that it has become imperative for me to cease for a shorter or longer period the very matters which have been conducted from truly heartfelt concern, namely, the personal consultations. Secondly — since mentioning only this does not give a full picture of things as they really are — I wish to say that for the future I release those friends who have had entirely personal conversations with me from any kind of need to preserve silence about matters they may have personally discussed with me. Whatever personal matters have been discussed between myself and any member can, although there is of course no obligation in this regard, be openly spoken about if the member in question so wishes. Everything that has ever taken place in the environs of anthroposophy can, if the members wish it, be made known to the entire world.

'This has become necessary because such really abominable things have been able to make their appearance in the environs of the anthroposophical movement. Those who really want to make progress esoterically will anyway be able to find opportunities for this; and I shall create a substitute for what is having to cease for the present. Just give me a little time for this. Ways and means will be found so that those who are treading the esoteric path — which they should continue to do quietly and energetically — will be able to find whatever it is they might need, even though for some time it will be necessary to desist from personal consultations because unfortunately this is the only way to help the anthroposophical movement remain afloat. Although with a heavy heart, this is the only way to combat the defamations which, like so much these days, are completely fabricated. There are so many people nowadays who not only distort but actually invent things for defamatory purposes.'

17 The lecture ended with the following words: 'In view of today's difficult circumstances I want to voice special thanks to our friends here at St Gallen, also on behalf of those who lead the anthroposophical movement. Despite difficulties with the hall and other circumstances they have enabled us to speak in public and also privately within the group in this town at this tragic time. Despite the obstacles they have enabled us to be together. For that our special thanks are due to all those dear friends here at St Gallen who have played a part in this.'

Lecture 3

1 In September 1898 R. Steiner was co-editor of the journal *Magazin für Litteratur* (Magazine for literature) with its drama supplement *Dramaturgische Blätter*. He wrote numerous articles for this journal. See the 5 volumes GA 29–33 of the Complete Works; also R. Steiner, *Autobiography. Chapters in the Course of My Life* (GA 28), Anthroposophic Press, Hudson 1999, Part Three.

2 Empress Elisabeth (1837–98). Consort of Emperor Franz Joseph I of Austria. She was stabbed to death in Geneva on 10 September 1898 by the Italian anarchist Luigi Luccheni.

3 It is not known who is meant.

4 See Lecture 2, Note 3.

5 For example R. Steiner, *The Mission of the Archangel Michael* (in GA 174a), Anthroposophic Press, New York 1961, lecture of 29 November 1915.

6 See Note 2 above.

7 Marie-François-Sadi Carnot (1837–94). Physicist, fourth president of the third French Republic, stabbed to death by the Italian anarchist Caserio.

8   See R. Steiner, *The Fall of the Spirits of Darkness* (GA 177), Rudolf Steiner Press, Bristol 1993, lecture of 7 October 1917.

9   See *inter alia* R. Steiner, *The Fall of the Spirits of Darkness*, op. cit.

10   See R. Steiner, *The Four Mystery Plays* (GA 14), Rudolf Steiner Press, London 1982, especially the final scene of 'The Souls' Awakening'.

11   Goethe *Faust*, II, Act 1, Gloomy Gallery, tr. A. G. Latham, London & New York 1935.

12   Ibid.

13   See R. Steiner, *Geisteswissenschaftliche Erläuterungen zu Goethes 'Faust'. Band II* (GA 243), Dornach 1981, lecture of 3 November 1917.

14   See Lecture 2, Note 12.

15   Goethe, *Faust*, I, Auerbach's Cellar in Leipzig, op. cit.

16   See R. Steiner, *The Riddle of Man*, op. cit., the chapter 'New Perspectives'.

Lecture 4

1   Lecture 3 in the present volume.

2   See Lecture 3, Note 9.

3   R. Steiner, *Anthroposophie und Naturwissenschaft. Geisteswissenschaftliche Ergebnisse über die Natur und den Menschen als Naturwesen* (GA 73), Dornach 1987, lecture of 12 November 1917.

4   See Ludwig Feuerbach (1804–72), German philosopher, in *Gedanken über Tod und Unsterblichkeit*, Stuttgart 1903, where the actual words are: 'Is that which the human being is something different from what he eats?'

5   The Swiss psychologist and philosopher Carl Gustav Jung (1875–1961), formerly a pupil of Freud, lived at Küsnacht near Zurich from 1909 where he practised privately as a psychoanalyst. From 1910 onwards he lectured at Zurich University. See R. Steiner, *Psychoanalysis and Spiritual Psychology* (in GA 178), Anthroposophic Press 1990, lectures of 10 and 11 November 1917; also *Anthroposophie und*

Naturwissenschaft, op. cit., lecture of 14 November 1917; also *Earthly Death and Cosmic Life* (in GA 181), Garber Communications Inc. 1989, lecture of 22 January; and *The Renewal of Education* (GA 301), Anthroposophic Press, Great Barrington 2001, the questions and answers following the lecture of 28 April 1920.

6 See Lecture 3 in the present volume.

7 See *inter alia* R. Steiner, *The Mission of the Individual Folk Souls in Relation to Teutonic Mythology* (GA 121), London 1970, lecture of 16 June 1910; also *Die geistigen Hintergründe des Ersten Weltkriegs* (GA 174b), Dornach 1994, lecture of 13 February 1915; and *The Karma of Untruthfulness*, Vol. I (GA 173), Rudolf Steiner Press, London 1988, lectures of 9 and 17 December 1916.

8 See Note 6 above.

9 Eliphas Levi (1810–75). Pseudonym of Abbé Alphonse Louis Constant. French esoteric writer.
Franz Xaver Benedikt von Baader (1765–1841. Physician, philosopher and theologist.
Louis Claude Marquis de Saint-Martin (1743–1803). French philosopher, theosophist and esotericist.

10 Here the lecturer added remarks similar to those at the end of Lecture 2 quoted in Note 16 to that lecture. He concluded with the following:
'Let those who find this unjust and feel that this means making the innocent suffer on account of the guilty please address themselves direct to the sources whence the defamations come.

'It is essential to get to grips with this now, otherwise matters will not improve within the Society. But they must improve. Total seriousness must spread throughout the Society, for it is the bearer of most important truths for the present time. I said today how sensitive one must be in spreading anthroposophical truths, and the Society must not be made to appear suspicious to our contemporaries by the appearance on the scene of certain individuals who always distort everything in the most infamous manner. I believe that those among our dear friends who take our task entirely seriously will be the ones who best understand the need for the disciplinary measures taken. I have to mention them here since I have already mentioned them in other groups and because I ask you to appreciate them appropriately. So far I have not found that the many remarks I have made in this matter have been taken sufficiently seriously; time and again the measures have been disregarded. Serious action is now needed, otherwise people will remain insufficiently aware of what is actually at stake.'

11   This refers to the lectures of 5, 7, 12 and 14 November 1917 in R. Steiner, *Die Ergänzung heutiger Wissenschaften durch Anthroposophie*, op. cit.

Lecture 5

1   See Lecture 4 in the present volume and R. Steiner, *Psychoanalysis and Spiritual Psychology*, op. cit., lectures of 10 and 11 November 1917.

2   R. Steiner, *Psychoanalysis and Spiritual Psychology*, op. cit., lecture of 10 November 1917

3   Ibid., lectures of 10 and 11 November 1917.

4   See R. Steiner, *The Occult Movement in the Nineteenth Century* (in GA 254), lecture of 11 October 1915, where the concept of the 'left-hand path' is defined more precisely: 'In occultism one is on the "left-hand path" if one aims to achieve a specific goal with the help of the occult teachings one represents. One is on the "right-hand path" in occultism if one is disseminating it purely for its own sake. Those treading the mid-way path aim to bring what our age needs by way of esoteric teaching for humanity at large out into the open and make it exoteric. Those, though, who stand very firmly on the left-hand path are the ones who combine specific in-

tentions with whatever occultism they disseminate. The degree to which one is on the left-hand path is measured by the dimensions of the specific purposes one is pursuing by leading people to the spiritual world and giving them all kinds of information from that world and by inoculating them in an improper manner with something which serves the sole purpose of realizing those specific goals.'

5 See Lectures 3 and 4 in the present volume and also Lecture 3, Note 8. Regarding the appearance of Christ in the etheric realm see, *inter alia*, R. Steiner, *The Reappearance of Christ in the Etheric* (in GA 118,130), Anthroposophic Press, New York 1983; also *Esoteric Christianity and the Mission of Christian Rosenkreutz* (GA 130), Rudolf Steiner Press, London 2000.

6 'The Portal of Initiation', see Lecture 3, Note 10.

7 See R. Steiner, *The Fall of the Spirits of Darkness*, op. cit.; also *Inner Impulses of Evolution* (in GA 171), Anthroposophic Press, New York 1984, lecture of 24 September 1916; and *Geisteswissenschaftliche Erläuterungen zu Goethes 'Faust'. Band II* (GA 273), Dornach 1981, lectures of 3 and 4 November 1917.

8 Ludwig Anzengruber (1839–89), Viennese writer: *Ein Faustschlag* (A blow with the fist), a drama in three acts, Act 3, Scene 6 literally: '. . . as truly as there is a living God! I am an atheist!'

9 See, for example, R. Steiner, *Inner Impulses of Evolution*, op. cit., lecture of 23 September 1916; *The Karma of Vocation* (GA 172), Anthroposophic Press, New York 1984, lecture of 27 November 1916; *The Karma of Untruthfulness*, Part I, op. cit., lecture of 26 December 1916; also *The Occult Movement in the Nineteenth Century*, op. cit.

10 See, *inter alia*, the lectures listed in Note 9.

11 See, *inter alia*, R. Steiner, *The Principle of Spiritual Economy* (GA 109), Anthroposophic Press & Rudolf Steiner Press, New York & London 1986.

12 See Lectures 6 and 2 in the present volume.

13 See R. Steiner, *Die Ergänzung heutiger Wissenschaften durch*

Anthroposophie, op. cit., especially the lecture of 7 November 1917.

14   See Lecture 2, Note 15.

Lecture 6

1   See R. Steiner, *Inner Impulses of Evolution*, op. cit.; *The Karma of Vocation*, op. cit.; and *The Karma of Untruthfulness*, Vol I, op. cit.

2   See Lecture 5, Note 4.

3   Wilhelm Wundt (1832–1920). German physician, philosopher and psychologist, founder of the first Institute for Experimental Psychology in Leipzig.

4   Fritz Mauthner (1849–1923). Bohemian writer and philosopher. He considered that Wundt 'owed it to his publisher' that he was seen as a classical writer on philosophy.

5   For example in Lectures 3 and 5 in the present volume. See also Lecture 5, Note 7.

6   See Lectures 3 and 4 in the present volume.

7   R. Steiner, *An Outline of Esoteric Science*, op. cit.

8   'The Portal of Initiation'. See Lecture 3, Note 10.

9   St Patrick (389–460), apostle and patron saint of Ireland.

10   See R. Steiner, *Die Ergänzung heutiger Wissenschaften durch Anthroposophie*, op. cit., lecture of 14 November 1917.

11   Thales of Miletus (*c.* 624/640–545 BC). Greek philosopher.

12   R. Steiner, *The Riddles of Philosophy* (GA 18), Anthroposophic Press, New York 1973, Chapter 'The World Conception of the Greek Thinkers'.

13   Frederick Winslow Taylor (1856–1915). American engineer, originator of time-and-motion studies in industry, founder of the Taylor System of scientific management: *The Principles of Scientific Management*, 1912.

14   See Lecture 1, Note 20.

Lecture 7

1   Professor Dr Martin Dibelius in an article 'Im vierten

Kriegsjahr' (In the fourth year of the war) in *Frankfurter Zeitung* No. 322, 21 November 1917.

2 See Lecture 4, Note 11.

3 See R. Steiner, *Approaches to Anthroposophy*, chapter 'Human Life from the Perspective of Spiritual Science' (in GA 35), Rudolf Steiner Press, Sussex 1992, lecture of 16 October 1916.

4 See Lecture 3 in the present volume. Also, e.g. R. Steiner, *Inner Impulses of Evolution*, op. cit., lectures of 24 September and 7 and 14 October 1916.

5 See R. Steiner, *The Karma of Vocation*, op. cit., lecture of 12 November 1916; *The Karma of Untruthfulness*, Vol. I, op. cit., lecture of 1 December 1916. Also *The Challenge of the Times* (in GA 186), Anthroposophic Press, New York 1941, lecture of 1 December 1918; and comments on John Worrell Keely and his invention, e.g. in *Toward Imagination* (GA 169), Anthroposophic Press, Hudson 1990, lecture of 20 June 1916. H. P. Blavatsky also devoted a chapter to this invention in her book *The Secret Doctrine. The Synthesis of science, religion and philosophy*. See also *Beiträge zur Rudolf Steiner Gesamtausgabe*, No. 107, Dornach, Michaelmas 1991: 'Der Strader-Apparat. Modell—Skizzen—Berichte' (The Strader machine. Model, sketches, reports).

6 See Lecture 6 in the present volume.

7 See R. Steiner, *Freiheit—Unsterblichkeit—Soziales Leben*, op. cit., lectures of 18 October and 23 November 1917. Also Lecture 1 in the present volume.

8 See R. Steiner, *The Fall of the Spirits of Darkness*, op. cit., lecture of 7 October 1917, and Notes 9 and 10 to this lecture.

9 Goethe, *Faust*, Part II, Act 2, Laboratory.

10 In *Critique of Practical Reason*, Part 1, Book 2, Main Section 2, Chapter VIII, Kant wrote of '... God, freedom and immortality...'

11 In his *Tagebücher* (Diaries) for September 1807, 7th paragraph, Goethe wrote of '...God, immortality and virtue...'

12 R. Steiner, *Freiheit – Unsterblichkeit – Soziales Leben*, op. cit., lecture of 18 November 1917.
13 Prentice Mulford, *The God in You. A Selection of Essays*, London 1917, which R. Steiner read in the German translation by Sir Galahad (pseudonym for Bertha Eckstein-Diener), Munich 1909.
14 In Lectures 6 and 1 in the present volume.
15 Lecture 3 in the present volume and Note 13 to that lecture.
16 Goethe, *Faust*, Part II, Act 1, Gloomy Gallery.
17 See Lecture 2, Note 12.

Index of Names

* = not mentioned by name

Anzengruber, Ludwig, 133*, 207

Baader, Franz Xavier Benedikt von, 119, 205

Carnot, Marie-François-Sadi, 86, 203
Columban, 66–7, 201*
Copernicus, Nicolaus, 1, 42, 45–6, 197

Darwin, Charles, 5, 35, 37, 173, 178, 193
Dewar, James, 15–16, 198
Dibelius, Martin, 175–6*, 187*
Du Bois-Reymond, Emil, 8, 198

Elisabeth Empress of Austria, 77*, 84*, 85–6, 203
Emerson, Ralph Waldo, 70, 201

Feuerbach, Ludwig, 112*, 204
Fichte, Johann Gottlieb, 12

Gall (St), 66–7, 71, 201
Goethe, Johann Wolfgang von, 40–2, 95*, 181, 182, 195*, 200, 209,
    210

Haeckel, Ernst, 35, 36–7, 199
Haller, Albrecht von, 41*, 200
Hartmann, Eduard von, 36–7

Hegel, Georg Wilhelm Friedrich, 12
Hertwig, Oscar, 37, 200

Kant, Immanuel, 17, 41, 182, 198, 209

Jung, Carl Gustav, 114*

Laplace, Pierre Simon, 17, 198
Levi, Eliphas, 119, 205
Luccheni, Luigi, 77*

Mauthner, Fritz, 161, 208
Mulford, Prentice, 186*, 210

Paracelsus, Theophrastus von Hohenheim, 62, 201
Patrick (Patricius), 168, 208

Saint-Martin, Louis Claude, 119, 205
Stinde, Sophie, 76, 152, 201

Taylor, Frederick Winslow, 172, 208
Thales of Miletus, 169, 170, 208

Vischer, Friedrich Theodor, 8, 11–12, 197, 198
Volkelt, Johannes, 8, 198

Wilson, Thomas Woodrow, 95, 195, 201
Wundt, Wilhelm, 161–2, 208

Note Regarding Rudolf Steiner's Lectures

The lectures and addresses contained in this volume have been translated from the German, which is based on stenographic and other recorded texts that were in most cases never seen or revised by the lecturer. Hence, due to human errors in hearing and transcription, they may contain mistakes and faulty passages. Every effort has been made to ensure that this is not the case. Some of the lectures were given to audiences more familiar with anthroposophy; these are the so-called 'private' or 'members' lectures. Other lectures, like the written works, were intended for the general public. The difference between these, as Rudolf Steiner indicates in his *Autobiography*, is twofold. On the one hand, the members' lectures take for granted a background in and commitment to anthroposophy; in the public lectures this was not the case. At the same time, the members' lectures address the concerns and dilemmas of the members, while the public work speaks directly out of Steiner's own understanding of universal needs. Nevertheless, as Rudolf Steiner stresses: 'Nothing was ever said that was not solely the result of my direct experience of the growing content of anthroposophy. There was never any question of concessions to the prejudices and preferences of the members. Whoever reads these privately printed lectures can take them to represent anthroposophy in the fullest sense. Thus it was possible without hesitation—when the complaints in this direction became too persistent—to depart from the custom of circulating this material "For members only". But it must be borne in mind that faulty passages do occur in these reports not revised by myself.' Earlier in the same chapter, he states: 'Had I been able to correct them [*the private lectures*], the restriction *for members only* would have been unnecessary from the beginning.'

The original German editions on which this text is based were published by Rudolf Steiner Verlag, Dornach, Switzerland in the collected edition (*Gesamtausgabe*, 'GA') of Rudolf Steiner's work. All publications are edited by the Rudolf Steiner Nachlassverwaltung (estate), which wholly owns both Rudolf Steiner Verlag and the Rudolf Steiner Archive. The organization relies solely on donations to continue its activity.

For further information please contact:

Rudolf Steiner Archiv
Postfach 135
CH-4143 Dornach

or:

www.rudolf-steiner.com

Rudolf Steiner
Evil
Selected Lectures

Despite the fact that evil is an omnipresent theme of our age, it remains one of the most problematic. Public references to it are continually made, but to what extent has society truly begun to understand its riddle?

In this selection of insightful lectures Rudolf Steiner addresses the subject of evil from the results of his spiritual research, offering an original and complex picture. He describes evil as a phenomenon which arises when a thing appears outside its true context, enabling something which is initially 'good' to become harmful. He speaks of the effect of particular spiritual beings—principally Lucifer and Ahriman—who work as polar forces, laying hindrances on our path. Yet, paradoxically, confronting and coming to terms with such difficulties ultimately furthers our development. Thus Steiner speaks of evil as a necessary phenomenon in human evolution, allowing for the possibility of freedom.

224pp; 21.5 x 13.5 cm; ISBN 1 855840 46 4; paperback; £11.95

Rudolf Steiner
Nature Spirits
Selected Lectures

Based on knowledge attained through his highly-trained clairvoyance, Rudolf Steiner contends that folk traditions regarding nature spirits are based on spiritual reality. He describes how people possessed a natural spiritual vision in ancient times, enabling them to commune with nature spirits. These entities—which are also referred to as elemental beings—became immortalised as fairies and gnomes in myth, legend and children's stories.

Today, says Steiner, the instinctive understanding that humanity once had for these elemental beings should be transformed into clear scientific knowledge. He even asserts that humanity will not be able to reconnect with the spiritual world if it cannot develop a new relationship to the elementals. The nature spirits themselves want to be of great assistance to us, acting as 'emissaries of higher divine spiritual beings'.

208pp; 21.5 x 13.5 cm; ISBN 1 855840 18 9; paperback; £11.95

Rudolf Steiner
Guardian Angels
Connecting with our Spiritual Guides and Helpers

Throughout the ages, traditional folklore has spoken of guardian angels as spirits who guide and protect human beings. In modern times, however, their existence has largely been written off as myth and superstition.

Based on his personal experience and cognition, Rudolf Steiner speaks of guardian angels and other spiritual beings as a reality. Their existence, he says, is a spiritual and scientific fact which can be fruitfully researched and studied through clairvoyant means. Furthermore, working consciously with these entities can assist each of us in fulfilling our evolutionary goals.

In these six specially selected lectures, Rudolf Steiner elucidates the role of the guardian angel, and also discusses our relationship to the heavenly hierarchies of spiritual beings as a whole, and how they shape our human form as a result of their cosmic activity.

144pp; 21.5 x 13.5 cm; ISBN 1 85584 073 1; paperback; £9.95

Rudolf Steiner
Guidance in Esoteric Training
From the Esoteric School

Selected from material given by Rudolf Steiner to members of his Esoteric School (1904–14), this volume features exercises, meditations and practices for spiritual self-development. In contrast to oriental methods of spiritual training, they derive from the western, Rosicrucian stream and are fully adapted to modern consciousness.

Various exercises are given—for morning and evening, for the days of the week and the months of the year. In addition, there is much explanatory material to deepen and enhance meditative work, including several articles on the path of inner development and the obstacles to be faced on the way to attaining true consciousness of the self.

This enlarged edition contains further clarification of the exercises, descriptions of the future evolution of the world and humanity, plus later advice given by Steiner on the nature of breathing exercises and ancient and modern methods of initiation.

192pp; 21.5 x 13.5 cm; ISBN 1 85584 076 6; paperback; £10.95